CLARENDON LIBRARY OF LOGIC AND PHILOSOPHY

General Editor: L. Jonathan Cohen, The Queen's College, Oxford

The *Clarendon Library of Logic and Philosophy* brings together books, by new as well as by established authors, that combine originality of theme with rigour of statement. Its aim is to encourage new research of a professional standard into problems that are of current or perennial interest.

General Editor: L. Jonathan Cohen, The Queen's College, Oxford.

Also published in this series

Philosophy without Ambiguity by Jay David Atlas
Quality and Concept by George Bealer
Psychological Models and Neural Mechanisms by Austen Clark
Sensory Qualities by Austen Clark
The Diversity of Moral Thinking by Neil Cooper
The Logic of Aspect: An Axiomatic Approach by Anthony Galton
Ontological Economy by Dale Gottlieb
Experiences: An Inquiry into some Ambiguities by J. M. Hinton
The Fortunes of Inquiry by N. Jardine
Metaphor: Its Cognitive Force and Linguistic Structure by Eva Feder Kittay
The Cement of the Universe: A Study of Causation by J. L. Mackie
The Nature of Necessity by Alvin Plantinga
Divine Commands and Moral Requirements by P. L. Quinn
Rationality: A Philosophical Inquiry into the Nature and the Rationale of Reason by Nicholas Rescher
Simplicity by Elliot Sober
Blindspots by Roy N. Sorensen
The Coherence of Theism by Richard Swinburne
Anti-Realism and Logic: Truth as Eternal by Neil Tennant
Ignorance: A Case for Scepticism by Peter Unger
The Scientific Image by Bas C. van Fraassen
The Matter of Minds by Zeno Vendler
Chance and Structure: An Essay on the Logical Foundations of Probability by John M. Vickers
Slippery Slope Arguments by Douglas Walton
What Is Existence? by C. J. F. Williams
Works and Worlds of Arts by Nicholas Wolterstorff

PLURALISM

Against the Demand for Consensus

NICHOLAS RESCHER

CLARENDON PRESS · OXFORD

Oxford University Press, Walton Street, Oxford OX2 6DP
Oxford New York
Athens Auckland Bangkok Bombay
Calcutta Cape Town Dar es Salaam Delhi
Florence Hong Kong Istanbul Karachi
Kuala Lumpur Madras Madrid Melbourne
Mexico City Nairobi Paris Singapore
Taipei Tokyo Toronto
and associated companies in
Berlin Ibadan

Oxford is a trade mark of Oxford University Press

Published in the United States by
Oxford University Press Inc., New York

First published 1993
First issued in paperback 1995

British Library Cataloguing in Publication Data
Data available

Library of Congress Cataloging in Publication Data
Rescher, Nicholas.
Pluralism: against the demand for consensus/Nicholas Rescher.
—(Clarendon library of logic and philosophy)
Includes bibliographical references and index.
1. Pluralism. 2. Pluralism (Social sciences). 3. Consensus
(Social Sciences) 4. Habernas, Jürgen—Contributions in concept of
consensus. I. Title. II. Series.
BD394.R47 1993 149—dc20 93-18392
ISBN 0-19-824062-7
ISBN 0-19-823601-8 (Pbk)

Printed in Great Britain
on acid-free paper by
Bookcraft (Bath) Ltd
Midsomer Norton, Avon

Preface

This book was conceived in early 1990 and sketched out during the summer of that year while I was visiting Oxford. It was then written in Pittsburgh during the ensuing academic year and polished in Oxford in the summer of 1991. However despite the Anglo-American setting of its production, the themes it deals with are primarily Continental, seeing that its primary target is the consensualism of Jürgen Habermas. The appeal of his canonization of consensus is strong but nevertheless so fraught with negative potential that it seems to me to deserve a forceful contradiction.

I am very grateful to Marian Kowatch and Annamarie Morrow for their patience in seeing the project take form on the word-processor through the course of numerous revisions. Jon Mandle read an early version of the manuscript and offered useful comments and suggestions. I am also indebted to Beth Preston for stimulating discussions of the issues, and for constructive criticism to L. Jonathan Cohen, John Kekes, and Tom Rockmore, as well as to an anonymous reader for the OUP.

N. R.

Pittsburgh, PA
September, 1992

For (though also against) Jürgen Habermas

*Philosophers do not write books to agree
with their colleagues. The best compliment
that they pay them is to take their work
seriously enough to react against it.*

Contents

Introduction

For much of the history of Western philosophy, consensus—uniformity of belief and evaluation—has been viewed as a desideratum whose ultimate realization can be taken as assured. Aquinas, in the Middle Ages, regarded consensus on fundamentals as a condition assured by *God*; Kant, in the eighteenth century, considered it as something rooted in the very nature of *Reason*; Hegel, in the nineteenth century, saw it as guaranteed by the spirit of cultivation working through the march of history ever enlarging its hold on human *Society*; Habermas in the twentieth century sees it as inherent in the very nature of *Communication* as an indispensible social praxis. Throughout much of the tradition consensus was viewed not just as something to be desired, but as something whose eventual actualization is effectively assured by some principle deep-rooted in the nature of things as we humans confront them in this world.

By contrast, many present-day writers invest social consensus not with confidence, but with hope. They look upon inter-personal agreement as a substitute for the assured verities of an earlier era in whose realization they have lost faith. Thus Thomas Kuhn, considering objective rationality to be an illusion, abandons the rational mandates of logical positivism to seek refuge in paradigms defined by community standards. Again, the 'strong programme' in the sociology of science of the Edinburgh school regards 'scientific progress' not as a matter of rationally validated knowledge but simply as one of group agreement forced under the pressure of political constraints. Various such currently popular tendencies of thought see rational standards as notable for their absence, with consensual opinion called upon to stand in their stead.

Either way, however, be it as inherent aspect of the human condition or as a prime requisite of societal well-being, consensus is accorded a centre-stage position in the rational scheme of things. The aim of the present book is to criticize this idea and to argue the case for abandoning the traditional endorsement of the centrality of consensus. The thrust of its critique of consensualism is twofold. Against dogmatic uniformitarianism, it seeks to defend a doctrine of pluralism in cognitive and social theory. But against the widespread current of relativistic indifferentism it seeks to defend the appropriateness of taking a committed and definite position, even in the face of views that differ from one's own. Accordingly, the stance advocated here is a pluralism that rejects both indifferentist relativism and dogmatic absolutism. Such a view seeks to occupy a middle ground between a traditionalistic rationalism that sees our cognitive and practical problems as admitting of only one possible solution dictated by reason alone, and a postmodern relativism that dissolves every sort of position into the indifferentism of personal interests, 'matters of taste,' group custom, or other such non-rational factors that can be mobilized in the interest of consensus formation.

In grounding its opposition to an insistence on the primacy of consensus, the present discussion emphasizes the paramount role of *interpretability* (rather than cognitive agreement) in matters of communication, and the paramount role of *acquiescence* (rather than practical agreement) in matters of social and political interaction. It thus prioritizes an epistemology of hermeneutics over one of consilience and a politics of live-and-let-live over one of conformity. From the angle of such a perspective, the critical fact is that be it in matters of inquiry or of praxis, co-ordination and co-operation are possible (and rational) even in the face of a disagreement of facts or values.

In line with this approach, the book presents a critical reaction against two currently influential tendencies of thought. On the one hand, it rejects the facile relativism that is widely pervasive in contemporary social and academic life. On the other hand, it opposes the aprioristic rationalism inherent in neo-contractarian theory—alike in the idealized communicative contract version promoted in continental European philosophy by Jürgen Habermas and in the idealized social-contract version of the theory of political justice promoted in the Anglo-American context by John Rawls. Against such tendencies, the presently envisioned pluralism takes a more realistic and pragmatic line that eschews the overly convenient recourse of idealization in cognitive and practical matters. In each case, so it is argued, the burden that consensus is asked to bear is more than can justifiably be placed upon it. And in each case there is much to be said—on grounds both of theoretical and of practical considerations—as to why an appropriate form of pluralism should be seen as preferable. The currently widespread penchant for consensus can be seen as the last stand in an ethos of democracy of a pre-democratic *dirigisme*—an insistence on social co-ordination that is unwilling to let people go their own way into a social diversification that affiliates each not to all but to such kindred spirits as circumstances may offer.

In contrast to a sanctification of consensus, the salient emphases of the present book are fourfold:

1. *Legitimate diversity*: the varying experiential situation of different people makes it normal, natural, and rational that they should proceed differently in cognitive, evaluative, and practical matters.

2. *Restrained dissonance*: a sensibly managed social system should be so designed that a general harmony of constructive interaction can prevail despite diversity, dissensus, and dissonance among individuals and groups—that differences can be accommodated short of conflict. This requires:

3. *Acquiescence in difference*: people can and should, to everyone's benefit, accept and come to terms with the idea—and the fact—that others will differ from themselves in opinion, in evaluation, and in customs and modes of action.

4. *Respect for the autonomy of others*: the rational and productive reaction to dissensus is not so much that we 'tolerate' others as that we respect their autonomy—that we concede their right to go their own variant way within the framework of such limits as must be imposed in the

interests of maintaining that peaceful and productive communal order that is conducive to the best interests of everyone alike.

Above all, the consensus-downgrading position articulated here opposes a utopianism that looks to a uniquely perfect social order that would prevail under ideal conditions. Instead, it looks to incremental improvements within the framework of arrangements that none of us will deem perfect but that all of us 'can live with'. Such an approach exchanges the yearning for an unattainable consensus for the institution of pragmatic arrangements in which the community will acquiesce—not through agreeing on its optimability, but through a shared recognition among the dissonant parties that the available options are even worse.

The fact is that we live in an imperfect world. The resources at our disposal are limited—our own intellectual resources included. We have to be prepared for the fact that a consensus among people, be it global or local in scope, international or familial, is in general unattainable. In a world of pervasive disagreement we must take recourse to damage control. We must learn to live with dissensus—with pluralism in matters of opinion. And we must *and can* bring to realization frameworks of social inclination that make collaboration possible despite diversity and that facilitate co-operation in the face of dissensus. In the setting of issues regarding social interaction, dissensus tolerance should prove positive and constructive. In the setting of issues regarding knowledge and inquiry it can, properly configured, lay the basis for a contextualistic rationalism intermediate between dogmatic absolutism on the one hand and relativistic nihilism on the other. The aim of the book is the development and substantiation of these rather ambitious claims. Its deliberations are undertaken in the belief that it is crucial for theoretical and practical purposes alike that we come to terms with the idea of an intellectual and social order than can function effectively even in the presence of dissensus.

I

Consensus, Rationality, and Epistemic Morality

1.1 *The Problem of Consensus*

Consensus is a matter of agreement. But people can of course agree or disagree on many different sorts of things—not beliefs and opinions alone, but also tastes, wishes, desires, goals, and so on. In particular, one must distinguish between agreement regarding what is to be thought, what is to be done, and what is to be prized. For consensus—agreement among diverse individuals or groups—can prevail in all three of these areas: the theoretical/cognitive, which is concerned with agreement or disagreement in matters of *belief*; the practical/pragmatic, which is concerned with agreement or disagreement with respect to *action*; and the evaluative/axiological, which is concerned with matters of *value*. All these issues clearly play a major role in the larger human scheme of things.

Two very different approaches to the prospect of disagreement and dissensus can be envisioned:

1. The consensualist: 'Do whatever is needed to avert discord. Always and everywhere work for consensus.'
2. The pluralist: 'Accept the inevitability of dissensus in a complex and imperfect world. Strive to make the world safe for disagreement. Work to realize processes and procedures that make dissensus tolerable if not actually productive.'

The first is a policy of dissensus avoidance; the second a policy of dissensus management. Now in this regard, it should be noted from the very outset that the present discussion will support the second, pluralist approach to our cognitive, evaluative, and practical affairs. Rejecting utopianism and unrealistic idealizations, its sympathies lie squarely on the side of accepting the realities of human disagreement and making of them the best that we possibly can.

The belief that consensus plays a leading role in matters of rational inquiry, decision, and evaluation is among the oldest and most pervasive ideas of philosophy. Consensus, various theorists have repeatedly urged, is somehow the touchstone of truth and the guarantor of correctness in matters of belief and of adequacy in matters of decision and action. Time and again, thinkers proceeding from very different points of view have reached the conviction that some sort of rationale or agency is at work that guides the community aright, at least over the long run. And in particular, from the early days of the subject in classical antiquity onwards, various philosophers have regarded communal agreement as a pivotal factor in the human quest for knowledge. There is good reason, however, to call into question this attractive but deeply problematic idea.

To be sure, there is a plausible rationale why theorists of knowledge should focus on consensus. As Kant maintained, all human judgement is personal judgement: 'I think' is omnipresent throughout its domain. Whatever belief or conviction in the truth of p that any one of us has and maintains can be recast as 'I think that p.' Be it in science or in common life, we can get at 'the truth' only through the mediation of what we think to be true; we have no direct way, independent of our beliefs on the issues, to get at the impersonal 'real truth of the matter'. Now in this context, consensus has a very important role to play. For its espousal represents a significant step beyond the potentially fractious views of individuals—a step not, to be sure, all the way to the level of *impersonal* objectivity, but at any rate to a level beyond that of subjective opinion. It replaces the 'I think' of the all too often idiosyncratic individual by the still, to be sure, mediated but now far less personalized and subjective 'we think' of the community. In so doing, we may or may not achieve the actual truth as such, but we do remove or at least diminish various sources of error, such as personal bias or individual carelessness.

There is thus much to be said on behalf of consensus as an epistemic touchstone. But, perhaps unfortunately, much can also be said against it. Wise leaders, after all, do not ask their advisers for a collective opinion from which all element of dissent has been eliminated: they realize that the interests of understanding are best served by a complex picture that portrays the state of existing information and speculation—and ignorance!—in its fully diverse complexity.[1] Dissensus and diversity can often play a highly constructive role in human affairs. It will, accordingly, be maintained here that contemporary partisans of consensus methodology seriously overestimate the need and desirability for according a central position to consensus, and that—in matters of inquiry and praxis alike—strong claims to cogency and appropriateness can be urged on behalf of a less consensus-oriented, more pluralistic approach.

1.2 *Is Consensus a Rational Imperative?*

In matters of inquiry, rational reflection or argumentation of and by itself certainly need not lead people to consensus—or to truth. For argument alone, however cogent, can only lead us to where our premises direct, so that we cannot take the line that truth lies on the side of the best arguments. (The more rigorous the argumentation, the more compelling is the principle: 'Garbage in, garbage out.') The extent to which we can place our confidence in what Jürgen Habermas calls 'the unforced force of the better argument' is thus limited. And no matter how widely accepted a contention on some significant issue may be, the prospect as often as not remains that some will (quite defensibly) dissent from it—a prospect that is virtually everpresent and ineliminable given the inevitable variation in people's information and situation.

When we disagree with another with respect to a certain thesis p, it is usually illuminating to examine the nature of the disagreement and to explore just what it is in this context that we do agree on. Thus consider the perfectly plausible prospect

[1] See the suggestive deliberations in Irving L. Janis, *Victims of Groupthink* (Boston, 1978).

of Table 1.1. Despite agreement on various categorical issues (q, r), the two parties differ regarding p because of their disagreement on implicational issues ($q \to p$, $r \to \sim p$). In so far as they have good reason to see such implicational linkages in a different light, a substantial agreement on categorical matters nevertheless leads the parties concerned in very different directions. And there is nothing inherently incongruous about a situation of this generic sort.

But must genuinely rational minds not ultimately reach agreement on meaningful issues? Does not the fact that rationality is inherently universalistic in its bearing—is objective and impersonal in its orientation—mean that rational people 'have to' attain a consensus, so that rationality remains absent where disagreement prevails? Not necessarily! For while in characterizing a resolution as rational we are indeed staking a claim that is universal in its substantive bearing and intent, it is nevertheless perfectly conceivable that there might not actually be a universal *consensus* about the matter. However plausible a non-truistic contention on any significant issue—rationality included—may be, the prospect that some people will (understandably and defensibly) dissent from it is ever present. The abstract thesis that 'Other things being equal, all rational people choose recognizably more effective problem-resolutions over less effective ones' is quite correct. But other things are seldom all that equal. And people of course can, given their different situations, quite appropriately disagree about what sorts of measures are effective. Rationality consists in effecting an appropriate alignment between our beliefs and the available evidence, but different individuals will generally confront different bodies of evidence and (in part for that very reason) will evaluate it differently.

TABLE 1.1.

A		B	
Accepts	Rejects	Accepts	Rejects
$q \to p$	$r \to \sim p$	$r \to \sim p$	$q \to p$
q		q	
r		r	
p		$\sim p$	

The idea that rationality as such necessarily leads to a consensus on substantive issues—let alone that it affords a sure road to the truth—is deeply problematic. It is simply mistaken to think that there must be a single appropriate answer to a factual question ('Who is the most prolific poet?'—are we to count lines or ideas?) or to a practical problem ('What is the best route to Paris?'—are we to prioritize time or distance?). The truth, no doubt, is one, but that fact does not preclude a diversity of justified beliefs about it. The situations where it lies in the rational nature of the case that sensible people must agree are comparatively few and far between. In general the rationality of judgements is not undermined as such by finding that there are some who dissent from them.

Reason enjoins us to do what is optimal as best we can determine it—what is the intelligent thing to do in the circumstances *as we discernibly confront them*, and so relative to the information *as we have it*. But the fact is that we are imperfect agents operating in an imperfect world. The most we can possibly do—and the most that can be asked of us in the name of rationality—is to do the best we can manage to do in the actually prevailing conditions. And here consensus seems to lie beyond our reach. Each of us, doing the very best we can in the inevitably different circumstances that confront us, is led in potentially separate ways. The long and short of it is that consensus appertains to rationality as an ideal, not as a realizable 'fact of life'.

Clearly there are some matters regarding which people *must* agree on pain of irrationality: for example, that one oneself exists; that there is a difference between truth and falsity; that people need food; that elephants are larger than mice. Agreed! Rational inquirers do—and should—agree on such matters. But just what is the significance of this linkage between rationality and such general agreement on certain obvious specifics? Its bearing on consensuality at large is, in fact, quite marginal. For these points of 'universal agreement among rational people' are not a matter of an ultimately discovered *de facto* universal consensus among people independently predetermined as rational. It is simply a matter of the meaning-standards that we who use this notion impose upon the idea of 'rationality' in the first place. We just would not accept as rational those who stand apart from the general view of matters of this sort. The 'consensus' that prevails among all rational people in such matters simply reflects the inevitable uniformity *that we ourselves predetermine by using our standards to determine who the rational people are.* The crux lies in a matter of conceptual circularity: we use the concept in a way that makes those truths truistic.

Disagreement with others confronts us with the problem of the source of disagreement. This ultimately lies in the fact that by nature and nurture people come equipped with different backgrounds of experience. And so, placed in circumstances of the same sort, different people are bound to respond differently.[2] It is all very well to invoke a principle of indifference to ground a rational uniformity of result. No one wants to deny that 'In *altogether identical* circumstances, rational people will arrive at *identical* results,' seeing that then there cannot (*ex hypothesi*) be any reason for preferring some other outcome. But the fact is that we do (or should) know that the variability of the human condition almost invariably precludes the realization of 'altogether identical circumstances'.

'But disagreement and dissensus is all too often rooted in mere ignorance.' True enough! But true in a way that provides no comfort to the partisans of consensus. Imperfect information is, after all, an inevitable fact of life. A 'rationality' that could not be implemented in these circumstances would be totally pointless. Were rationality to hinge on possessing complete information, it would thereby manifest its irrelevance for the human condition. There is nothing 'mere' about 'mere ignorance': it is an ineliminable feature of the human situation.

To be sure, someone might press an objection along the following lines:

---

[2] John Rawls's notorious supposition, in his *A Theory of Justice* (Cambridge, Mass., 1971), that rational agents will *ipso facto* respond uniformly in hypothetically identical conditions (and in particular in the 'original position' of a social contract made 'behind the veil of ignorance') simply ignores the realities of the human condition. The adult human mortal is not—cannot be—a *tabula rasa*.

One can unproblematically accept the idea of a *substantive* dissensus as being compatible with rationality—and indeed as being demanded by it in circumstances where different bodies of evidence are involved. But *methodological* consensus—agreement on the methods and procedures for evaluating the evidence and its implications—is surely a demand of reason.

This line of reasoning does, however, encounter some very serious obstacles. There are many areas of investigation in which the methodology–substance distinction can accomplish useful and necessary tasks. But the domain of knowledge itself is not one of them. When the questions at issue belong to the theory of knowledge and inquiry, matters become so intricately intertwined that any prospect of a neat substance–methodology separation becomes impracticable. (The reason is that we can only learn about the comparative efficacy of methods through trial and that learning from experience is itself a cognitive matter.)

Consensus as such is neither an indispensable means to, nor a necessary effect of, people's commitment to rational cogency. For we have to come to terms with the realities, which include:

1. The diversity in people's experiences and epistemic situations.
2. The variation of 'available data'.
3. An underdetermination of facts by data.
4. The variability of people's cognitive values (evidential security, simplicity, etc.).
5. The variation of cognitive methodology and the epistemic 'state of the art'.

Such factors make for a difference in the beliefs, judgements, and evaluations even of otherwise 'perfectly rational' people. Short of an implausible hypothesis of a biological and situational cloning that equips every one of a community of inquirers with exactly the same cognitive basis for opinion-foundation, it is clear that a consensus among its members will not be attainable.

Rationality can be counted upon to lead to truth with categorical security at best only under ideal—and thus effectively unrealizable—conditions.[3] And it leads to *consensus* only in situations of uniform experience—which are, obviously, also not generally realized. In the circumstances in which we labour in this world, consensuality is neither a requisite for, nor a consequence of, rationality in the conduct of inquiry—it is neither a necessary nor sufficient condition for it. Nor is it a practicable goal.

But does abandoning a demand for consensus not make rationality itself into something variable and culture-dependent? By no means! Disagreement means no more than that the ideal of rationality must be pursued and cultivated—within those groups and cultures that pursue and cultivate it at all—in circumstance-conditioned and therefore person-variable ways. To be sure, rationality as such is self-identically uniform. *What rationality is* is something that is fixedly defined by the conception itself—by the item that constitutes the topic of discussion. However, variation enters in with considerations regarding *what is rational*, seeing that different people operate in different circumstances. Rationality is in this regard like communication. What communication is is the same everywhere and for everyone—inherent in the nature of the concept that is at issue. But, of course, it is only normal and natural that different people in different places and times would transact their communicative business very differently, since what is effective in one context may fail to be so in another. Similarly, *what rationality is* is one thing (and one uniform thing from person to person within the framework of a meaningful discussion of this particular topic); but *what is rational* is something else again—something that is by no means uniform from person to person but variable with situation and circumstance.

Consider the prospect of regulative principles of rational process along such lines as:

1. Only adopt methods that effectively militate towards consensus.
2. Only adopt methods that are bound to produce consensus under mutually favourable conditions.

---

[3] See ch. 2, 'Truth as Ideal Coherence', of the author's *Forbidden Knowledge* (Dordrecht, 1987).

All such rules envisage as a methodological requirement a condition that is neither requisite for, nor necessarily conducive to, the realization of our cognitive goals. The paramount desideratum in this connection is not the achievement of agreement as such, but rather the avoidance of specifically harmful and damagingly counter-productive forms of dis-agreement.

The question, 'which takes priority, rationality or consensus?' accordingly has to be answered by putting rationality in the first place. In this regard, Jürgen Habermas is quite right. For he correctly and properly insists on distinguishing a *de facto* consensus (*faktisch erzielte Konsensus*) which may root in a fortuitous concurrence, from a rational consensus (*vernünftige Konsensus*) that is strictly and entirely the product of people's implementing the norms of reason. However this right-minded stipulation on Habermas's part has unfortunate implications for his own theory of the consensus–rationality relationship. For if *this* is the sort of approach we take, then the move from consensus to rationality is indeed right and proper—but also *trivial*. We cannot now clarify rationality in consensual terms without vitiating circularity, seeing that we need to have recourse to rationality in explicating the sort of consensus that is to be at issue. What Habermas's theory of consensus ultimately demands is not just any old consensus, but a consensus produced through an adherence to rational principles. What counts for him is consensuality reached 'solely by force of cogent argumentation'. And then we can extract rationally from consensuality all right, but only because we put it there in the first place.

We can get rationality out of Habermas's idealized consensus because we have been instructed to pack rationality into it. But we might then just as well have started from a concern for rationality as such and left consensus out of it. For now consensus is merely something ornamental, something that does no real work for us. The whole complex story of consensus pivots on rationality, and all recourse to the process of opinion formation is now a fifth wheel that spins idly while rationality is doing the real work. Injunctions like 'Promote the formation of consensus' or 'Do not stand outside an emerging consensus' have to be interpreted in this light. Such injunctions to consensus only make sense when the burden of obligation is born not by consensuality as such, but by whatever it is that makes the consensus at issue a good one (the true, the rational, the right, etc.). From the angle of rationality it will only be a rationally engendered consensus that is significant: and what is significant about it is not its consensuality but its rationality. Once it is acknowledged that it is *rational* consensus that matters and not consensus as such, any prospect of extracting rationality from consensus in a meaningful, non-circular way has to be abandoned.

1.3 *Do the Limitations of Reason Demand Consensus?*

Centrality of consensus can also be argued from a rather different point of departure—one that pivots the issue on the limitations of human reason. This line of thought goes back to the Sophists of ancient Greece. The human mind, so they maintained, is a weak and limited instrument. Our reason and our language (*logos*) cannot grasp reality—they are too impotent to capture the real truth of things. The crux lies in distinguishing what is by custom (*nomos*) and what is by nature (*phusis*). For language and logic are themselves the creation of custom, designed not to put the minds of men in touch with physical reality but to put them in touch with one another. But while reality as such is something extra-human that lies beyond the reach of our inadequate cognitive grasp, human discourse conventions are thought-things that we ourselves make and hence can understand and come to terms with. People would—all of us—live as isolated individuals in our own private world of personal experience and personal thought if we did not make use of the artefacts of language to break out of this isolation by coming to agreement, by co-ordination and compact, by employing custom (*nomos*) to provide by convention and consensus for a lawful conformity that nature (*phusis*) itself does not supply. Rationality itself accordingly roots in consensus. Or, to put it differently, since rational insight into the real is beyond us, it is consensus that provides us with the functional equivalent that is the best we can, in the circumstances, manage to achieve in the direction of truth and knowledge. Real, capital-K Knowledge (*epistēmē*) being unavailable, communal consensus is the most and the best that we can achieve in its place.

The present-day exponent of this sort of doctrine is Richard Rorty's new-model pragmatism: 'the doctrine that there are no constraints on inquiry save conversational uses—no wholesale [i.e. global] constraints derived from the nature of the objects, or of the mind, or of language, but only retail [i.e. local] constraints provided by the remarks of our fellow inquirers'.[4] Any effort to validate community-transcending standards or criteria is nothing but an attempt to 'escape from history'. There is no such thing as an objective validity or cogency that reaches beyond the domain of opinion; the best we can do is to find a confluence of opinion, a consensus. Any notion of cogency of reasoning or plausibility of contention reflects a hankering after unattainable, opinion-transcending absolutes. Community standards are our only subjectivity-transcending resource. Consensus in these matters of inquiry and question resolution is the pivotal factor because it represents the best and the most that we can possibly hope to achieve. It is at once the touchstone of epistemic practicability and of epistemic validity. We are led to a recourse to consensuality not because of its inherent attraction and power but simply *faute de mieux*. Consensus is a *substitute* for an inherently unavailable rationality.

The salient defects of this sophistical position were already noted by Socrates in his polemic against Protagoras. Consensus is no effective substitute for cogency because there can be good as well as bad consensus—agreement that is evil or stupid as well as agreement that is benign and wise. Agreement as such need not lead to any destination worth attaining—1,000 people can be just as wrong-headed (or wrong-minded) as a single individual. When a consensus confronts us that is not the end of the matter but the beginning. For we are then well advised to ask *why* that consensus exists: is it a matter of mere mindless conformity, or of knuckling under to the powerful, or is it a matter of the weight and presence of the evidence and the merit of the case?

---

[4] Richard Rorty, *Consequences of Pragmatism* (Minneapolis, 1982), 165.

It is never *just* consensus we want but the *right sort* of consensus—that is, a consensus produced in the right way—one that obtains for good and cogent reasons. And then we are back to putting rationality at the base of it.

1.4 *Is Consensus a Moral Imperative?*

To this point, it has been argued that there is no good and sufficient reason for seeing rationality to consist in, or indeed even as merely to be committed to, a quest for consensus. But the question remains open whether the pursuit of consensus—despite such *epistemic* limitations—may nevertheless not be a matter of *moral* obligation. Is it perhaps a valid ethico-moral imperative that we should strive to establish consensus with others by endeavouring to achieve a meeting of minds with them?

Suppose for the moment that consensus were to be accepted as a valid social goal, so that people-in-general should properly strive for consensus, on the ground of there being a collective social obligation to work for its realization. What would this mean for duties at the level of the individual agent?

Two alternatives confront us in this regard. To bring X and Y together we can move X towards Y or Y towards X (or do some of both). And so, in the present case, the imperative to consensus allows of two possible implementations. On the one hand there is the perspective: 'I should always be prepared to compromise my opinions for the sake of moving them closer to other people's. I have a pervasive duty to try to conform my opinions to those of others.' On the other hand we obtain: 'I have a duty to evangelize other people towards my own opinions, to endeavour to convert others and gain their adherence to my own beliefs.' Barely to contemplate such modes of consensus-promotion is to see the untenability of this whole line of approach.

The fact is that consensus can be bought at too dear a price. In general terms, we face a situation of choice between two very different sorts of consensus promotion:

1. Expending our efforts and resources in an endeavour to bring others around to our own convictions,

2. Compromising our opinions so as to align them with those of others.

And over against consensus-seeking there stands the contrasting policy of letting things stand as they are, with us persisting in our own views and others continuing to hold theirs. Now from the aspect of rationality, the choices that confront us here should be addressed through a sensible balance of benefits against costs. And here the outcome of such an assessment will vary from case to case. There is simply no assurance to be had on the basis of abstract general principles that the resolution will inevitably favour consensus.

When I realize that my position on some issue of consequence disagrees with yours, I am well advised to inquire into *how* it is that you have rendered a conclusion different from mine—and presumably then to change my view if the grounds for yours appear to be stronger. But I am not well advised to worry about the bare fact *that* your beliefs differ from mine in ways that are detached from the issues that relate to grounds and reasons. It makes good sense to revise beliefs to accommodate them to other *evidence*, but it makes no rational sense to revise them to accommodate other *people*. It is sensible to take account of the beliefs of others and—above all—of their reasons for their beliefs. But it is nowise obligatory for me to accommodate my beliefs to theirs independently of this. In opinion formation our duty is surely not towards a co-ordination with others as an independent desideratum of its own, but simply towards the truth. The obligations we have in this regard involve such principles as 'Do all you can to form your opinions on the basis of rationally cogent grounds,' and 'Stand by your opinions when formed on this basis irrespective of where other people stand.' The sensible posture is that we should strive to assure the rational cogency of our opinions and let consensus look after itself. The insistence on consensus—on the comforting assurance of group solidarity—is an understandable but at the same time problematic sign of adolescence and immaturity: 'To realize the relative validity of one's convictions [or—as I would prefer to say—their *limited acceptability*] and yet stand for them unflinchingly, is what distinguishes a civilized man from a barbarian,' one wise observer of the human condition tells us.[5]

In various sorts of circumstances, people do indeed have a moral obligation towards the truth—to find out what it is and even to assert it by giving it a public voice. But such an obligation comes down to a matter of intellectual honesty—to seek out and to express the truth as we see it in so far as this may be appropriate to the situation. And this is something very different from a commitment to pursue consensus as such. Our commitment to the truth may possibly lead us to agree with others and lead others to agree with us. But this is something subsidiary and incidental. The intellectual honesty that may (or then again may not) lead to agreement undoubtedly constitutes a valid moral obligation. But agreement as such—for its own sake irrespective of such other moral desiderata as candour or honesty—is not something to which we are morally obligated.

Morality unquestionably calls for seeing others as entitled to their views—their disagreement from ours notwithstanding. There is a substantial, and for present purposes highly important, difference between *respecting* someone and *agreeing* with them. To respect others is to regard them as the bearers of appropriate rights and entitlements and is—as such—a requisite of benign coexistence. But due respect certainly does not require agreement. On the contrary, it requires a recognition of others as autonomous agents entitled ·to go their own way irrespective of our approval or disapproval, agreement or disagreement. And to respect another person as such is to do more than merely to *tolerate* them; it is to see them as units of worth and bearers of rights and entitlements in view of their shared status as rational creatures. But none of this calls for *agreeing* with them by making our ideas give way to them or by belabouring them in the interest of leading them to put their ideas into conformity with ours. Morality, in sum, calls on us to respect the views of others. But this has nothing to do with *agreement*. On the contrary, it has to do with seeing value in the messenger

[5] Josef Schumpeter as quoted in Isaiah Berlin, *Four Essays on Liberty* (Oxford, 1969), 172. See p. 243 of Schumpeter's *Capitalism, Socialism, and Democracy*, 3rd edn. (New York, 1950).

despite our discordant views as to the correctness of the message.[6]

Indeed, far from agreement with others being the focus of a moral obligation, it would seem that the call of moral duty works rather differently. It is, after all, an important aspect of morality that we should respect the autonomy of ourselves and of others—that in our own case self-respect demands that we should maintain due respect for others requires that we should concede a person's right to go their own way. At some point, people have a right to stop listening to me, and, contrariwise, I am entitled to insist that they let me be—however much they may think me wrong. From this moral point of view, we have no right to press for consensus past a certain point of valiant effort, and we have every responsibility to recognize mature and responsible people as autonomous agents fully entitled to shape their own views irrespective of any disagreement with ours.

There is, however, yet another aspect of the issue of the linkage of consensuality to morality—an aspect that is inherent in a line of thought also at work in the writings of Habermas—namely the move, not from morality to consensuality, but, rather, conversely, from consensuality to morality. This line of thought is reflected in a line of argumentation characterizing what this philosopher calls 'discourse ethics'.[7] Here the first premiss has it that the requirements of consensus (which is inherent in the quest for the truth) can be properly served only through a well-managed communal inquiry—a rationally conducted discussion. And the second premiss has it that a well-managed inquiry (or rationally conducted discussion) requires adopting certain fundamental principles of morality (namely, fairness, candour, a sharing of information, respect for the ideas and judgement of others, and the like). In consequence, so the

[6] To be sure, where the interests of third parties are involved, the 'duty to respect people's opinions' is limited by the morality of concern for their best interests. If Smith lies ill in the street and you think we should say incantations rather than summoning a physician, it would be reprehensible of me to 'be a good fellow' and go along with you for the sake of agreement.

[7] See Habermas's essay, 'Discourse Ethics: Notes on a Program of Philosophical Justification', in C. Lenhart and S. W. Nicholsen (eds.), *Jürgen Habermas: Moral Consciousness and Communicative Action* (Cambridge, Mass., 1990), 42–115.

argument has it, a commitment to consensus carries in its wake a commitment to morality (and to inherent principles for furthering the common good).

But this Habermasian conception of a consensualistic grounding of ethics is deeply problematic. For consensus as such can be the product of morally questionable means—it can be constrained on by *force majeure* or induced by indoctrination. It is only if we load morality into the particular sort of consensuality that we favour that the transition from consensuality to morality will be unproblematic. But then, of course, the argumentation becomes circular, because if we put rationality and morality into consensuality, then it is an unsurprising—but also uninformative—result that we can get rationality and morality out of consensuality. In such conditions we can extract moral lessons from the conditions of consensuality only because we have insisted on focusing on the good sort of consensuality in the first place. The fact is that when Habermas represents his 'discourse ethics' as providing for a 'programme of philosophical justification' of morality this justificatory programme is fundamentally flawed, seeing that it is only because he fixes upon a good (rationally and morally appropriate) mode of consensus that Habermas is able to extract ethical import from a commitment to its pursuit.

2

Is Consensus Required in the Pursuit of Truth?

2.1 *The Philosophical Partisans of Cognitive Consensus*

In every era of philosophical history consensus has found prominent exponents and advocates.

Aristotle. Aristotle stands first and foremost among the major figures in whose thought consensus has played a prominent role. His theory of knowledge distinguished emphatically between strictly scientific knowledge (*epistēmē*) and the less rigorously grounded information that serves the purposes of everyday life. And Aristotle placed consensus squarely in the second category, maintaining (in bk. I, sect. 16 of the *Topics*) that the authority of a significant consensus constitutes an adequate basis for warranted belief, and affirming in the *Nicomachean Ethics* (bk. X, sect. 2; 1173^{a}1) that 'that which every one thinks actually is so'. But he held that for scientific knowledge something more is required—namely, rational demonstration. Consensus thus provides a validation for claims—albeit not by way of their authentication as genuinely scientific knowledge (*epistēmē*), but by way of their substantiation as cognitively appropriate belief (*pistis*). In this way, premisses adequate for the inferences and reasonings of everyday life situations become available through a consensus of informed people (either everyone, or the appropriate experts or, at least, the majority of people). In this way, as Aristotle saw it, consensus enjoys an important albeit subordinate status in the epistemic scheme of things—a status which, although not one of ultimate authority, is at least one of substantial weight.

St Augustine. Like Aristotle before him, St Augustine assigned the topmost place to *reason* as being our paramount resource in matters of theory. But consensus—so he taught—holds sway in matters of authority, those of religious authority included. *Securus iudicat orbis terrarum.* God would not let his people go astray and wander in random groping without cognitive guides in matters where reason does not settle the issue. With Aristotle, Augustine thus gives to consensus a significant role in the formation of rational opinion. And along lines similar to those suggested by Cicero earlier on,[1] Augustine saw 'general agreement' or 'common consent' (*sensus communis*) as one of the cornerstones for the validation of religious belief.

The Enlightenment. Enlightenment thinkers of the era of Condorcet and Laplace envisaged a rational evolution towards an ultimate condition in which rational knowledge and reality stand in co-ordinated conformity. The salient idea is that human thought is involved in an inexorable process moving towards an ultimate rationally engendered comprehension of the nature of the real. The formation of a consensus among cultivated people is the eventual upshot of the unfolding of this co-ordinating operation of human reason.

J. S. Mill. The very differently motivated doctrine of John Stuart Mill's *On Liberty* is actually not altogether dissimilar from that of Hegel in its ultimate results. Mill too assumes a fundamentally progress-invoking position. He envisions natural developmental impetus towards the definitive truth: There is a present of strife and conflict; a developing future during which the better stepwise overpowers the worse; and an ultimate, eventual future in which consensus reigns because the truth has conquered. Accordingly, free rein should be given here and now to intellectual conflict and controversy because—in the end—the correct position will overcome all the rest in free and open competition. Unfettered rivalry and competition among conflicting opinions and ideas is a means to progress because it is through such conflict that

---

[1] Cicero endorsed the principle *Omni autem in re, consensio omnium gentium lex naturae putanda est* (*Tusculan Disputations*, 1. 13. 30 ff. and compare 1. 41. 36) and *De quo autem omnium natura consentit, id verum esse necesse est* (*De natura deorum*, 1. 17, and cf. 2. 2). He used this principle to establish the existence of the gods.

the truth will ultimately emerge and prevail. The power of the truth is so compelling that it will ultimately produce agreement among its sincere devotees. (An important corollary of this view is that any societally enforced limits on the freedom to form, hold, and advocate beliefs is counter-productive, because it impedes the natural process through which an ultimate consensus on true belief can ultimately emerge. This is the crux of Mill's argument for 'tolerance' in *On Liberty*.)

C. S. Peirce. In the face of the philosophic sceptic's agnosticism regarding the very possibility of attaining 'the real truth' about nature, Peirce proposed that in these matters *the truth is simply 'the limit of inquiry', that is, what the scientific enterprise will discover in the idealized long run*—or would discover if the efforts were so extended.[2] The truth is nothing but the ultimate consensus of the community of scientific inquirers: once scientific progress reaches a point at which a question is answered in a way which is thereafter maintained without change within the ongoing community of inquirers, then it is indeed the true answer to the question in hand.[3] A 'Copernican inversion' reminiscent of Kant is at issue in this Peircean approach: it is not that rational inquiry is appropriate because what it ultimately arrives at is the actual truth, but rather that 'the actual truth' qualifies as such just exactly because rational inquiry ultimately arrives at it:

[R]eality, the fact that there is such a thing as a true answer to a question, consists in this; that human inquiries—human reasoning and observation—tend toward the settlement of disputes and ultimate agreement in definite conclusions which are independent of the particular stand-points from which the different inquirers may

---

[2] If 'life and mental vigor were to be indefinitely prolonged', as he puts it in one passage (*Collected Papers*, 8. 41 (*c*.1885)). Again, 'Truth is that concordance of an abstract statement with the ideal limit towards which endless investigation would tend to bring scientific belief' (ibid. 5. 565 (1901)).

[3] We need not, however be parochial and conceive of 'the ongoing community of inquirers' as necessarily limited to human beings: 'We may take it as certain that the human race will ultimately be extirpated . . . But, on the other hand, we may take it as certain that other intellectual races exist on other planets,—if not of our solar system, then of others; and also that innumerable new intellectual races have yet to be developed; so that on the whole, it may be regarded as most certain that intellectual life in the universe will never finally cease' (ibid. 8. 43 (*c*.1885)).

have set out; so that the real is that which any man would believe in, and be ready to act upon, if his investigations were to be pushed sufficiently far.[4]

On such a view, the truth about factual matters at the level of theoretical generality can be identified with what science will maintain in the long run. Knowledge of nature's laws, our attainment of 'the real truth' about the world, can thus be construed as being what Peirce characterized as the 'final irreversible opinion' of the scientific community.[5] Scientific truth is a matter of ultimate consensus—the truth here simply *is* 'the opinion which is fated to be ultimately agreed to by all who investigate'.[6] For Peirce (and it is this aspect of his thought that particularly appeals to Jürgen Habermas) the truth is something fixed precisely because there is an ultimately decisive *method* of question-resolution (measurement paradigmatically, but by extension the entirety of scientific method)—a method of such a sort that anyone and everyone who uses it conscientiously and persistently must ultimately arrive at the same fixed result. Where this is not so, there simply would be no 'truth of the matter'. Factual truth and long-run consensuality are inherently co-extensive.

Josiah Royce. Peirce geared consensus to an ultimately emergent community of scientific inquirers. Extending this approach in his book *The Problem of Christianity*, Royce projected the conception of an idealized community. Our individualized fragmented, temporarily divided selves are envisioned as somehow capable of being fused into a single unified community—a cohesive whole 'acting as if we could survey in one single unity of insight that wealth and variety

---

[4] *Collected Papers*, 8. 41 (*c*.1885).

[5] For Peirce, science is effectively a latter-day surrogate—a functional equivalent, as it were—for the medieval philosopher's conception of the 'mind of God'; idealized long-run science is infallible with respect to nature (thesis 1), and is moreover omniscient with respect to nature (thesis 2). ('I should say that God's omniscience, humanly conceived, consists in the fact that knowledge in its development leaves no question unanswered' (*Collected Papers*, 8. 44 (*c*.1885).) The real truth about factual matters, on such a view, simply coincides with what science maintains to be so in the long run, and so genuine knowledge can be construed as final irreversible opinion.

[6] Ibid. 5. 407 (1878). In the essay 'What Pragmatism Is' (ibid. 5. 416–34), Peirce proposes 'to define the "truth" as that in a belief to which belief would lead if it were to tend indefinitely toward absolute fixity'.

and connection which, as a fact, we cannot make present to our momentary view' (p. 267). Royce supposed an innate human impetus to intercommunication as the prime instrument of community formation. Royce calls the basic form of community a community of interpretation, the defining characteristic of such a community being a 'will to interpret'—a purposeful endeavour on the part of the members to grasp each other's ideas and interpret them to one another. This purpose cannot be perfectly fulfilled in any actually realized human community, but it can be approached and approximated. And what is approximated in this way is an Absolute—a theoretical construct that is the matrix of perfected thought (be it descriptive or evaluative). The conception of this Absolute affords the yardstick by which the incompleteness and imperfections of our divided fragmentary thoughts about reality must be appraised. In Royce's theory, the shared insight of such an idealized consensus of a 'perfect community' provides the definitive standard of truth and value.[7]

Jürgen Habermas: Consensus as a Regulative Principle of Rationality. Habermas is the theorist who has in recent years most emphatically and cogently envisioned a central position for consensus in human praxis—and has, indeed, made the quest for consensus a foundation-stone of his philosophy. Habermas co-ordinates communication with a quest for consensus. As he sees it, human communication is based on an implicit commitment to an 'ideal speech situation' the envisioning of which is 'the constitutive condition of rational speech' and which thus serves as 'the normative foundation of agreement in language'. And this ideal speech situation is one in which all the parties involved are committed to a search for consensus—albeit a normative consensus produced by rationally cogent reasons and the 'peculiarly unforced force of the better argument'.[8] Habermas accordingly views the commitment to a search for consensus as an integral, constitutive

---

[7] For a compact overview of Royce's position see Elizabeth Flower and Murray G. Murphey, *A History of Philosophy in America* (New York, 1977), 750–3, and Bruce Kuklik, *The Rise of American Philosophy* (New Haven, Conn., 1977), 391–3.

[8] Jürgen Habermas, 'Wahrheitstheorien', in *Wirklichkeit und Reflexion: Festschrift für Walter Schulz* (Pfüllingen, 1973), 258–9 (repr. in G. Skirbekk, ed., *Wahrheitstheorien* (Frankfurt am Main, 1977)).

component of the communicative impetus inherent in human rationality. Where the ancients *contrasted* consensus with reason, and in consequence accorded consensus a subordinate place, Habermas sees the impetus to consensus as the constitutive core of rationality itself.

In line with this perspective, Habermas maintains that it is essential to individual and social rationality to forge and strengthen the conditions under which this realization of consensus is facilitated. He insists that a deeply unsatisfying (indeed profoundly irrational) state of affairs obtains when the parties to a discussion abandon the quest for a common ground and give up the determination to pursue consensus. For him, to abandon the quest for consensus is to abandon rationality as such. Consensus thus emerges as the ruling desideratum of rational inquiry and the issue of conduciveness to its attainment becomes the governing standard of cognitive rationality. The salient evaluative question in this regard is: 'Does the process at issue facilitate or hamper the movement towards a consensus?' To be sure, Habermas regards the pusuit of consensus less as a practical objective than as a regulative principle, a guiding ideal. It is a normative guide rather than a practically realizable condition—a telos that determines regulatively, procedurally, methodologically the way in which we are to conduct our cognitive business if we are to proceed rationally. What is at issue is something of a Kant-reminiscent 'categorical imperative' of rational inquiry: 'Proceed as if engaged in a communal co-operative venture whose ultimate ruling aim is to arrive at consensus.'

As even so brief a survey of the historical lie of the land makes clear, the Enlightenment was a watershed in thinking about the role of consensus in the epistemic scheme of things. For the ancients (Aristotle and Augustine) consensus was a *supplement* to theoretical reason which provides for resolutions in matters that this instrumentality itself cannot settle. But the moderns—from Enlightenment days to Habermas—envision consensus as the product and result of the workings of reason. They are, one and all, emphatically unwilling to acknowledge probative weight to any cognitive resources apart from reason, the sole source of legitimate consensus.

Another noteworthy aspect of modern consensus epistemology in the recourse to *idealization* that is manifested alike in Peirce's resort to 'the ultimate community of inquirers' as it will eventually emerge in the theoretical long run, in Royce's invocation to the ideal of a 'perfect community', and in Habermas's emphasis on the *regulative* aspect of the matter. For such theories agree in dismissing consensus as it may be established here and now as a force of probative weight. Instead, there is a radical shift in the nature of the consensus. A factually constituted community—one that includes everyone now living or, say, every adult, or every speaker of the language—is an *empirical* reality. But a *normatively* constituted community—or say, one that includes 'all right-thinking people', or 'all rigorous and persistent inquirers', or the like, is something rather different. For it is clear that since the consensus of a normatively constituted community is itself something of a fundamentally evaluative nature, that is not something that can be regarded as a merely descriptive, 'value-free', evaluatively neutral conception. If concepts like 'truth', 'correctness', 'rationality', and the like are construed with reference to the situation of an ideal (perfected, completed) community, then they wear their normative character on their sleeves. And such recourse to idealization in an appeal to consensus accordingly makes a great difference when one confronts the question: 'Why should people feel called upon to endorse a consensual position?' For the work of evaluation is presupposed as an already accomplished fact whenever an *evaluatively* constituted consensus is at issue. (A normatively geared consensus is unavoidably to some extent question-begging when such normative issues are under consideration.)

In any case, our historical perspective indicates that consensus has three distinct aspects, as set out in Table 2.1. Historically, the allegiance of the partisans of consensus has been moving down the list, with most recent consensus theorists placing their reliance on consensus on a mutually idealized interpretation of the issue. Mill and Peirce have us look to eventual consensus, so that the concern for consensus takes on an eschatological view. Royce and Habermas stress the regulative and idealized dimension. Thus the modern

TABLE 2.1. *Modes of consensus*

1. *De facto* consensus as present here and now in the community ('of all' or 'of the knowledgeable experts').
2. *Ultimate consensus* as it will (presumably) come to exist in the community, in the eventual future ('the long run').
3. *Idealized consensus* as a hypothetical eventuation that would be reached under ideal (though doubtless never actually realizable) conditions.

partisans of consensus would have us enter into the realm of millenarian thought in a distancing from the workaday realities that removes the reliance on consensus ever further away from the level of accomplished facts.

2.2 *The Critics of Cognitive Consensus*

Notwithstanding its many and eminent partisans, theorists who reject any and all appeal to consensus in matters of fact and value have never been lacking. We shall consider, in particular, three major groups, sceptics, cognitive élitists, and social science critics.

Sceptics. Sceptical philosophers since the days of classical antiquity have flatly rejected the appropriateness of an appeal to consensus in matters of the true or the right. As they see it, we humans have no prospect whatsoever of validating claims, and even consensus would be totally inconclusive in this regard. There is no *royal* road providing access to secure truth, and no *communal* road either. For Sextus Empiricus and his congeners, the community is just as liable to error as is the individual. The ancient sceptic's assault on the idea that universally conceded principles are *ipso facto* correct was renovated in John Locke's *Essay Concerning Human Understanding*, which insists (bk. I, ch. 2) that even such near truisms as 'Whatsoever is is', or 'It is impossible for the same thing to be, and not to be', 'are so far from having a universal assent that there are a great part of mankind to whom they are not so much as known'. The real issue, as Locke emphasized, is not universal assent as such, but universal assent among the genuinely knowledgeable (sect. 17). And even here the question remains wide open whether such assent carries any probative force in validating the actual truth of beliefs. Francis Bacon may speak for the whole tribe of traditional sceptics on this point:

True consent is that which consists in the coincidence of free judgements, after due examination. But far the greater number of those who assent . . . have addicted themselves thereto from prejudgement and upon the authority of others; so that it is a following and going along together, rather that consent. But even if it had been a real and widespread consent, still so little ought consent to be deemed a sure and solid confirmation, that it is in fact a strong presumption the other way. For the worst of all auguries is from consent in matters intellectual . . . For nothing pleases the many unless it strikes the imagination, or binds the understanding with the bands of common notions, as I have already said. We may very well transfer, therefore, from moral to intellectual matters the saying of Phocion, that if the multitude assent and applaud, men ought immediately to examine themselves as to what blunder or fault they may have committed.[9]

The problem, of course, is that consensus does not bridge over the truth–opinion divide that has been on the agenda of philosophy ever since the days of Parmenides. A consensus as such is still no more than a consensual *opinion* that reflects the beliefs of the group. There may be safety in numbers, but they afford no guarantees.

Cognitive Élitists. Yet another group of philosophers who reject the quest for consensus are those who might be called cognitive élitists. Their first spokesman was Heraclitus of Ephesus. Heraclitus distinguished humanity's common *capacity* for reason from the imperfect *exercise* of this capacity, which can produce bizarre misunderstandings even in entire communities. He taught that: 'It is necessary to follow "the common"; but although reason (the *Logos*) is common, the many live as though they had a private understanding' (Frag. 195).[10] Whether individually or collectively, people just are not all that rational: 'For although all things happen according to reason (the *Logos*), men act like people of no

---

[9] *Novum Organum*, 1. 77.

[10] In G. S. Kirk, J. E. Raven, and M. Schofield, *The Presocratic Philosophers*, 2nd edn. (Cambridge, 1983).

experience . . . [and] fail to notice what they do after they wake up just as they forget what they do when asleep' (Frag. 194). The great majority have a befuddled understanding; they fail to realize the truth and do not recognize that 'the real constitution of things is accustomed to hide itself' from the careless observation of 'the many' (Frag. 208). Heraclitus accordingly saw no need to give credence to the views of the herd, and viewed consensus as devoid of probative value.

The most prominent disciple of Heraclitus in this matter of disdaining the general consensus was Plato, who also emphatically rejected the idea that credence should be given to the views of 'the many'. He insisted, in the *Republic*, that only a small, select, and trained élite can be expected to achieve insight into the truth of things. Most people are content simply to amuse themselves with shadows whose underlying basis in reality is beyond their grasp.

Plato and Heraclitus thus inaugurated a tradition of cognitive élitism that has found its adherents in every place and era. On a such a view of the matter, what the consensual opinion of people-in-general ('the common herd') deserves is not respect but scornful rejection. Insight belongs to the few, not the many.

Social Science Critics. In point of empirical fact, people's dedication to consensus has its limits. Even when inquirers form an attachment to a favoured 'school of thought' they seldom stick by it through thick and thin. The indications are that if people cannot reach agreement relatively quickly in deliberating about matters of fact, then the chances of their not doing so at all increase dramatically with time. (See Table 2.2.) Additional interaction becomes increasingly unlikely to produce agreement; at some point, further discussion becomes unprofitable.

Considerations of this sort indicate that an insistence on actually achieving consensus is not really very practical. But with the rise of the 'social sciences', objections to the quest for consensus have come to be equipped with a more formal theoretical basis. Considerations of deep-rooted general principle were now called upon to reveal grave problems about using majority opinion as a touchstone of truth. An early example of this approach is M. J. A. Condorcet's

TABLE 2.2. *Statistics on hung juries in a study of 2,001 trials of 1–10 days in length*

Total hours of deliberation	% of total deliberations	% of these deliberations failing to reach a unanimous verdict
0–1	55	1
1–2	19	8
2–3	10	10
3–4	6	11
4–5	4	24
5+	6	30

Source: Harry Kalven, Jr., and Hans Zeisel, *The American Jury* (Chicago, 1966), 459.

TABLE 2.3.

	1	2	3
A	+	+	−
B	+	−	+
C	−	+	+

argument against the internal consistency of majority opinion. He observed that it is perfectly feasible that a majority should endorse each one of a group of mutually incompatible beliefs, such as the following:

1. Plato is wiser than Aristotle.
2. Aristotle is wiser than Socrates.
3. Socrates is wiser than Plato.

Concretely, in a hypothetical group of three individuals, *A*, *B*, and *C*, the acceptance situation with respect to those contentions might stand as in Table 2.3. Such situations are perfectly possible and self-consistent. But note that here the majority consensus endorses *all* those theses at issue. And these, being inconsistent overall, cannot possibly represent truth. The 'consensus' yielded by majority opinion is not a rational one.[11]

A comparable situation obtains when matters of probability are at issue. Consider, for example, a lottery with 100,000

[11] Cf. Duncan Black, *The Theory of Committees and Elections* (Cambridge, 1958), for an examination of various problems of this sort.

tickets. Vast majorities will agree that 537 will not come up. And exactly the same will hold for any other *particular* number. But if we proceed to settle questions of truth on this (probabilistically guided) majoritarian basis, then the resultant body of 'truth' will be collectively inconsistent.[12] Again, 'consensus' procedures cannot yield a rationally satisfactory result.

The 'Arrow Paradox' encapsulated in the economist Kenneth J. Arrow's famous Impossibility Theorem is yet another case in point.[13] The argumentation at issue demonstrates that when, in situations of choice, several inherently plausible requirements are set for forming a collective group consensus from the distributive preferences of individuals, then no rationally viable process of consensus formation will be available at all. Theoretical obstacles to forming a 'social aggregate' from an amalgamation of individual opinions thus indicate the infeasibility—as a matter of fundamental principle—of forming an appropriate preference-consensus mechanism. (And it does not matter whether the preferences at issue are preferences for action or preferences for thesis-acceptance; if the move from individual to collective preference is problematic, then what holds for the goose of action holds for the gander of belief as well.)

The fact is that recent times have seen a distinct divergence of thought on the issue of consensus. Twentieth-century philosophers of consensus have widely argued the merits of an *idealized* conception of consensus, while its twentieth-century social-science critics have generally argued against its *practical* unattainability and untrustworthiness as a general-purpose resource. In principle these views are, of course, quite compatible. It is, after all, perfectly possible that consensus, while unattainable in practice, is nevertheless a meaningful theoretical ideal. Moreover, even though consensus may fail us as an all-purpose instrument, it is perfectly possible for it to

[12] The lottery paradox was originally formulated by H. K. Kyburg, Jr., *Probability and the Logic of Rational Relief* (Middletown, Conn., 1961). For an analysis of its wider implications for inductive logic see R. Hilpinen, *Rules of Acceptance and Inductive Logic* (Amsterdam, 1968; *Acta Philosophica Fennica*, fasc. 22), 39–49.

[13] For a philosophically informed account of the relevant issues see Alfred F. MacKay, *Arrow's Theorem: The Paradox of Social Choice* (New Haven, Conn., 1980).

play an important, *limited* role in the conduct of our cognitive affairs in more narrowly defined, special-purpose contexts. Let us pursue this line of thought.

2.3 *Modern Limited Defences of Consensus*

Notwithstanding the problems of a larger ideology of consensus, it will prove informative to examine some examples of limited, special-purpose cognitive roles for the pursuit of consensus.

Scientific Methodologists. In science—and, above all, in the natural sciences—the quest for consensus is a well-established *desideratum*, manifested in the scientific community's insistence on two interrelated consensus-geared desiderata. The first is the *reproducibility of experiments*, subject to the stipulation that only those observations are qualified to furnish scientifically acceptable data which can be repeated and reconfirmed by other investigators; only those experiments merit endorsement as providing scientifically usable results which reproducibly and uniformly yield one and the same generally obtainable outcome. The second desideratum is the *verifiability of claims*, subject to the requirement that scientifically appropriate reasonings (inferences and calculations) must be described in sufficient detail that any qualified investigator can retrace and recheck independently the argumentation on whose basis a given conclusion is advanced. Both of these factors of observational and ratiocinational robustness provide strong impetus to consensus. Their insistence on public (i.e. investigator-indifferent and repeatable) data and inferences means that those conclusions which the community accepts at all it will accept in common. Impersonally cogent consonant and convergent processes of observation are insisted upon as crucial for scientific authenticity because they are instrumentalities of consensus. In ways such as these, communal acceptance represents a touchstone of viability in science.[14]

---

[14] A clear statement of this position is presented in Keith Lehrer and Carl Wagner, *Rational Consensus in Science and Society* (Dordrecht, 1981), see esp. pp. 7–8. It should be observed, however, that the significance of consensus in science is limited by considerations to which we shall shortly turn.

Epistemic   Minimalists. Winston   Churchill   remarked   that democracy is the worst form of government—except for all the rest. Even so, one might regard the consensus method as representing the worst process of question-resolution, except for all the rest. Such a position would concede to its various critics the theoretical difficulties of consensuality, but yet dismiss them as substantially irrelevant for its role in practice. To be sure, its advocates will not base this endorsement of consensus on the claim of a special communal power, an insight to be attributed to the group along the lines of the idea that 'the world spirit guides the community aright'. On the contrary, the justifying rationale roots in a sense of limitation and impotence. The line of supporting argumentation is roughly this, that exactly because no definitive source of right guidance has been granted to us mere mortals, the community judgement is the best we can do, since by accepting it we minimize discord and dissension engendered by conflict and disagreement. Thus the envisioned legitimation of a reliance on group consensus does not root in a *theoretical advantage* but in its affording a *practical compromise* along the lines of least resistance.[15]

Cognitive   Psychologists. Human   cantankerousness   notwith-standing, juries tend to reach agreement. People exhibit an inclination to form beliefs that meet the approbation of others. Thus an investigation that examined more than 280 jury deliberations revealed not one instance in which a hung jury was caused by a single dissenter.[16] Unless someone who disagreed with the majority was supported by at least one other colleague, dissenters invariably relaxed their reservations and came around to the majority view.

Noting such phenomena, psychologists have repeatedly

---

[15] Historically, the idea of consensus plays a particularly central role in the law, with its traditional concern for the opinions and interpretations prevalent among the accepted authorities. Thus the doctrine of *communis opinio* plays an important part in canon law, and the historical formation of a *herrschende Meinung*, a prevailing opinion in the profession and the wider community, has long been an important consideration in legal theory and practice. See Rita Zimmerman, *Die Relevanz einer herrschenden Meinung für Auwendung, Fortbildung und wissenschaftliche Erforschung des Rechts* (Berlin, 1983).

[16] See Harry Kalven, Jr. and Hans Zeisel, *The American Jury* (Chicago, 1966), 462-3.

confirmed a tendency among extensively interacting people to move their opinions closer together. But does such a tendency to opinion-convergence in interacting groups move any closer to the truth? Empirical investigations of this question afford interesting indications that indeed they do—that in very straightforward factual matters, at any rate, collectively formed group opinions are generally more closely 'on target' than the mere mechanical average of individual opinions. On the basis of such findings, Olaf Helmer and his collaborators have devised a formal process of interative feedback for the formation of group opinion—a process that has come to be known as the Delphi Method.[17] Moreover, various experiments in this area indicate that group opinions on straightforward factual issues arrived at by such interactive processes of opinion formation tend to move in the direction of the 'right' answer, and that consensus judgements will (in such matters) be more reliable than the mere average of the separate, individual opinions of group members. To be sure, the range of circumstance for which this has been substantiated is limited in its scope to somewhat simple-minded situations. It would clearly be too mechanical a view of inquiry to hold that those and only those processes can be trusted as truth-producing which yield the same consensual result irrespective of who employs them—be they talented or incompetent, genius or idiot.

Moreover, the impetus to consensus in matters of inquiry is a knife that cuts two ways. Several recent studies illuminate the extent to which we actually depend upon others in shaping our belief. The experiments of Solomon Asch have dramatized people's tendency to conform to erroneous public judgements on matters where they would never make mistakes by themselves.[18] His subjects had only to specify which of three lines was closest in length to a given line. People made this judgement unerringly, except when they saw that their

[17] For a description of this methodology and an indication of relevant literature see Olaf Helmer, *Looking Forward* (Beverly Hills, Calif., 1983).

[18] Specifically, Solomon Asch found that in certain situations of interactive estimation, 'whereas the judgements were virtually free of error under control conditions, one-third of the minority estimates were distorted toward the majority'. See his 'Studies of Independence and Conformity: i. A Minority of One Against a Unanimous Majority', *Psychological Monographs: General and Applied*, 70 (1956).

companions, who were asked the same question, concurred (by covert pre-arrangement) in giving a different answer.[19] Commenting on Asch's experiments, Sabini and Silver report:

All (or nearly all) subjects reacted with signs of tension and confusion. Roughly one-third of the judgements subjects made were in error. Nearly 80 per cent of the subjects gave the obviously wrong answer on at least one trial. The perception that a few other people made an absurd judgement of a clear, unambiguous physical matter was a very troubling experience, sufficient to cause doubt, and in some cases conformity.[20]

Such studies clearly reveal the impetus towards consensus as a mechanism that also has a considerable negative potential for leading people away from the truth.

Meaning Theorists. A common consent theory of *meaning* seems perfectly correct and innocuous. How the words and symbols that we deploy in communicating are to be used will clearly depend on the patterns of practice indigenous to the community within which they are employed. Clearly, words mean what their users agree upon: on issues of use and meaning, communal consensus is the appropriate and final arbiter. Here there is no room for any further issue of right/wrong, proper/improper, correct/incorrect over and above the matter of conformity to the communicative norms of communal practice.

So far so good. But following the track of this line of thought, some epistemic theoreticians incline to the idea that the intimate interrelation between truth and meaning brings it about that a consensuality semantics of meaning carries a consensuality epistemology of truth in its wake. This view is very questionable, to say the least. In general, once we have settled what a sentence or other linguistic construct *means*— what claim (thesis, statement, proposition) it asserts—the question of the *truth* of whatever has been asserted still remains wide open. And it is perfectly clear that this is generally something above and beyond the issue of communal practices—an issue not to be settled by communal consensus, but one that hinges on 'the facts of the matter'.

---

[19] *Psychological Monographs: General and Applied*, 69.

[20] John Sabini and Maury Silver, *Moralities of Everyday Life* (Oxford, 1982), 84–5.

To be sure, there will be some special cases in which issues of truth and meaning are so closely interrelated that settlement of the latter issue carries that of the former in its wake. But these cases of 'purely conceptual' truth—where a statement's truth status can be settled simply with reference to the very meaning of the terms at issue in its formulation—involve special circumstances that complicate an otherwise plain, straightforward story. In the main, and certainly in all substantively factual cases, issues of meaning generally do not settle questions of truth. ($2 + 2 = 4$ differs crucially from 'The cat is on the mat.') The consensual conventionality of linguistic and of mathematical truth—if conventional and consensual it is—would not engender that of truth in general. The pivotal role of consensus/convention in the domain of *formal* truth (in logic, linguistics, and mathematics) is surely not a model for the epistemic situation in general—one that applies even in the non-formal, factual domain. The consensuality of meaning is thus a fact of a limited epistemic bearing; it does not expand into a larger essentiality of consensus in matters of rationality at large.

With this survey of limited cases of consensus-utility concluded, let us return to the larger issue of the appropriateness of a commitment to consensus in cognitive matters in general.

2.4 *Science and Consensus*

Two sorts of situation standardly confront us in inquiry and information processing. The one obtains in *inductive* inquiries where the scanty evidence at our disposal *underdetermines* the answer to the questions we have in hand, so that various alternative answers are possible. The other sort of situation obtains in *reductive* inquiries where the surfeit of information at hand *overdetermines* the answer to our questions through inconsistency, so that once again alternative resolutions are possible. In either event, people's substantivity-laden epistemic standards ('criteria of plausibility') will come into play in such a way that a diversity of answers—a dissensus, in short—will arise. Quite plausibly, and without any rational inappropriateness, different cognitive agents can—given their various backgrounds of experience—resolve the issues variantly on account of different emphases among pertinent standards and criteria.

The ground rules of rational process (in scientific method, commonsense conjecture, and the like) by which we try to resolve our factual questions do not of themselves suffice—in general—to constrain a consensus on the basis of whatever data are *unproblematically* available. The available mechanisms of rational resolution leave room for some element of judgemental variation. Even intersubjectively shared methods and procedures need not lead to a uniform result when employed by those whose experience differs. (The same processes of extrapolation lead to different results when applied to the different bodies of data available to different invetigators.)

To be sure, in contexts of rational inquiry people generally take various measures to minimize such invitations to diversity-inherent informative under- or over-determination. In particular, in the natural sciences we demand the robustness of measurements, the reproducibility of experiments, and the verifiability of measurements. In the mathematical sciences we demand the effectiveness of demonstrations and checkability of calculations. Are not these indications of a striving for consensus?

They are certainly indicative of such an aspiration. But it is one that sensible people expect to be realized in practice only to a very limited extent. For those consensual processes in matters of cognition are in the end no more than useful devices for eliminating or reducing *mistakes* of various sorts—mathematical calculating errors, for example, or experimenter bias. They are not so much mechanisms for assuring truth as safeguards against various particular sources of error. And since the elimination of error makes only a partial contribution to the discovery of truth, their operation leaves ample scope for disagreement and diversity.

To be sure, the scientific community does often achieve substantial consensus on issues of concrete particularity—for example, on the response to questions such as: 'What is the atomic weight of lead?' or 'What is the speed of light?' But such detail-oriented consensus on measurable specifics does not generally extend to a broader theoretical domain. And the reason for this is not difficult to see, since theories are always *extrapolations* from the 'hard data'.

In the 1969 Postscript to his important book, *The Structure of Scientific Revolutions*,[21] Thomas Kuhn emphasized the role of the shared values of the scientific community. The 'paradigms' which lie at the centre of his analysis are seen as the products of community consensus, dictated by the customs of the group through the operation of shared beliefs and values. Indeed, as Kuhn sees it, the scientific community is *constituted* as such on the basis of such consensual commitments. The fact, however, is that this emphasis on communal consensus in science needs to be qualified. For one thing, as Kuhn himself makes clear, such consensus is certainly not stable. Scientists in different periods certainly differ regarding even basic values. (Take chance and chaos, for example: against the quantum theorists, Einstein imaged a God who does not play dice with the universe.) Moreover, the scientific controversies of the day constantly manifest value diversities. (One need look no further than current debates over evolutionary theory for examples of this phenomenon.)

The fact is that science is not an inherently consensual business: controversy is all too common in this domain. It is well known that facts underdetermine theories, and the theoretical interpretation of agreed facts always leaves scope for disagreement. The accession of 'new truths'—new scientific information—inevitably engenders the opening up of new questions: scientific change over the course of time relates not only to what is 'known' but also to what can be *asked*. In natural science the answer to existing questions always opens up further questions and leads us into new areas of uncertainty and disagreement. As science 'progresses' we do, no doubt, achieve the equilibrium of a consensus on some issues, but this equilibrium is an unstable one because generally as we push our inquiries more deeply we encounter further unresolved and inherently controversial problems. At and near science's creative edge there are always disagreements. Putting astronauts on the moon did not end controversies over its origin; it shifted the areas of dispute, but did not diminish them. The

---

[21] Thomas S. Kuhn, *The Structure of Scientific Revolutions* (Chicago, 1962), 135.

progress of science sees the unfolding of an ever-widening area of agreement. But with the opinion of the field as a whole, the area of *disagreement* also increases.

Throughout the areas near a research frontier there are always controversial issues that divide the community into conflicting and discordant schools of thought. And the rivalry between such schools is one of the main goads and incentives to the productive efforts of scientific researchers, each school being eager to validate its hunches and to vindicate its point of view. Dissensus is prevalent throughout science and provides one of the main stimuli to scientific progress. Far from science being a domain pervaded by consensus, there is, in fact, good reason to think that dissensus and controversy are the lifeblood of scientific work at and near the frontiers of research—though, to be sure, the rational *and social* dynamics of scientific opinion formation does generally make for an eventual uniformization of scientific opinion. Disagreement is in fact so pervasive and prominent a factor in science that it seems plausible to see dissensual debatability as a standard of value, and to regard a scientific question as important and interesting precisely in so far as there is room for disagreement about it.

Although it seems tempting to take the view that 'the scientific method' somehow of and by itself is consensus-engendering, that is a deeply dubious proposition. After all, very different formations of 'science' can—and have—existed. Epistemologists have often said things to the effect that people whose experience of the world is substantially different from our own are bound to conceive of it in very different terms. Sociologists, anthropologists, and linguists talk in much the same terms, and philosophers of science have recently also come to say the same sorts of things. According to Thomas Kuhn, for example, scientists who work within different scientific traditions—and thus operate with different descriptive and explanatory 'paradigms'—actually 'work in a different world'.[22] It is (or should be) clear that there is no simple, unique, ideally adequate concept-framework for 'describing the world'. The botanist, horticulturist, landscape gardener, farmer, and painter will operate from diverse cognitive 'points

[22] Thomas S. Kuhn, loc. cit.

of view' to describe one selfsame vegetable garden. It is mere mythology to think that the 'phenomena of nature' can lend themselves to only one correct style of descriptive and explanatory conceptualization. Different cognitive perspectives are possible, no one of them more adequate or more correct than any other independently of the aims and purposes of their users.

Immanuel Kant's insight holds: there is good reason to think that natural science as we know it is not something universally valid for all rational intelligences as such, but a cultural artefact. We have little alternative to supposing that our science is limited precisely by its being *our* science. The inevitability of empiricism—the fundamentality of experience for our knowledge of the world—means that our scientific knowledge is always relativized ultimately to the kinds of experiences we can have. The 'scientific truth' that we discover about the world is *our* truth, not so much in the sense that we make it up, but rather in the sense that it reflects our technologically available modes of interaction with nature.

The development of a science—a definite codification of the laws of nature—always requires as input some inquirer-supplied elements of determination. The result of such an interaction depends crucially on the contribution from both sides—from nature and from the intelligences that interact with it. A kind of 'chemistry' is at work in which nature provides only one input and the inquirers themselves provide another—one that can massively and dramatically affect the outcome in such a way that we cannot disentangle the respective contributions of nature and the inquirer. Things cannot of themselves dictate the significance that an active intelligence can attach to them. Human organisms are essentially similar, but there is not much similarity between the medicine of the ancient Hindus and that of the ancient Greeks.

Natural science—broadly construed as inquiry into the ways of nature—is something that is in principle endlessly plastic. Its development will trace out a historical course closely geared to the specific capacities, interest, environment, and opportunities of the inquirers that develop it. We are deeply mistaken if we think of it as a process that must follow a route generally parallel to ours and issue in a roughly comparable product. It would be grossly unimaginative to think that either the journey or the destination must be the same—or even substantially similar.

What makes for consensus among the scientists of the day is not just (and perhaps not even primarily) the inherent rationality of 'the scientific method' seen as a bloodless abstraction of rational process. Rather, it lies in the operation of the social processes of the inquiring community. Scientists are impelled to consensus less by an intersubjectively rational methodology than by a conformism imposed by promotion committees, funding agency appraisers, and peer review boards. Yet even these pressures, though powerful, achieve only limited uniformity of thought in an area where innovation and novelty are of prime value.

Admittedly, a potent dose of idealization can help matters. There is little room (and little need) to object to the idea that 'the (real) truth' is what ideally rational people would agree on in ideal epistemic circumstances (complete information etc.). But for one thing this is totally unhelpful, since it provides us with no real guidance for the conduct of inquiry. And—more seriously yet—the idea of consensus actually does no useful work here. We might just as well say: 'The (real) truth is what an ideally rational *individual* investigator would maintain in ideal epistemic circumstances.' The ideal consensus aspect then falls out (as a cost-free consequence) of one's commitment to the objectivity (impersonal validity) of *the (real) truth* as the product of rationality perfected.

The long and short of it is that even in scientific investigation we cannot expect consensus to prevail. Precisely because empirical inquiry, rationally conducted, requires the alignment of question-resolving theory with experience, we have to face the implication of the fact that different inquirers living in different times and circumstances are bound to have different experiences. And these different experiences are not just likely but actually *bound* to lead them to different destinations which in their very nature preclude the agreement requisite for a consensus. Ironically, it is not an indifference to the truth but the seriousness of their dedication to it that impels differently situated inquirers into dissensus.

In various respects consensus is doubtless a good thing. The impetus to consensus unquestionably resonates to the human predicament: it reflects our penchant for conformity and our deep-rooted inclination to accept what others do, so as to achieve the comforts of solidarity and companionship. Moreover consensus can, in some conditions, provide us with the reassurance of being on the right track. But be this as it may, consensus is not something on which we should insist so strongly as to make it a pervasive imperative for current concern. A universal consensus fixed upon 'the truth of the matter' or 'the optimal course of action' is not a practical goal but merely a hopeful aspiration. It is one of those things the achievement of which we would doubtless welcome but the actual pursuit of which as a practical goal makes no real sense.

Agreement among rational inquirers across the separating divides of time and place is not something that often (let alone necessarily) happens in the real world. The diversity of persons, cultures, and experiences makes the goal of actually realizing consensus in cognitive or evaluative practical matters effectively impracticable and unrealistic. Only by abstracting from the physical and social realities—by shifting to the level of idealization—can we require or expect a valid consensus.

As far as rational inquiry is concerned, then consensus is no more (but also no less) than a 'regulative ideal' in Kant's sense. It is something we would ideally like to have, abstractly speaking, but which we do not expect to achieve in the concrete situations in which we actually labour. Consensus may be a gleam in our eye that reflects our scientific aspirations, but it does not influence the reasonable expectations with which flesh-and-blood inquirers can reasonably proceed in their workaday endeavours.

3

The Problems of a Consensus Theory of Truth

3.1 *What Constitutes Consensus?*

Just what is it that constitutes a consensus? Clearly consensus consists in widespread and pervasive *agreement*. But exactly what is agreement anyhow? This simple-seeming question has more complexities than meet the eye of first view.

Take matters of belief. You think that what John is talking about is a cat. I happen to think it is a dog. Can it be said without further ado (and, in particular, without our being explicitly asked) that we agree that a domestic animal is at issue? You think Marlowe wrote *Hamlet*; I think it was the Earl of Warwick. Are we *agreed* that it wasn't William Shakespeare—or his cousin Reginald of whom we have never even heard? Does a correctly deduced point of commonality among beliefs automatically thereby constitute a point of agreement—irrespective of what the parties literally accept? After all, at some point of abstraction there is always a seeming 'agreement'. I think *p*, you think *q*. It is then clear that both of us are logic-bound to endorse *p*-or-*q*. But this 'agreement' surely cuts no ice for a serious consideration of matters of consensus regarding beliefs. Again, consider matters of evaluation. If you regard the Democratic candidate alone as acceptable, and I view the Republican as the only viable possibility, does that mean we are *agreed* that the Vegetarian candidate is unacceptable—even where we may not actually be aware that one was running?

The most plausible view here is to take the line that 'agreement' only exists where a question on the agenda of relevant questions is answered by both of us in the same way. And this makes the issue hinge crucially on exactly what the question-agenda happens to be. If the agenda consists of the being equal, all rational people choose recognizably more Marlow) and I (who think it was the Earl of Warwick) simply do not agree. There is just no consensus of any sort. After all, 'Not Shakespeare' does not appropriately answer the question 'Who wrote Hamlet?' On the other hand, if the question agenda consists of 'Did Shakespeare write Hamlet?', then both of us—each of whom answers negatively—indeed *are* in agreement (notwithstanding our rather different views on the matter). The crux is that the question of agreement/ disagreement and consensus/dissensus is crucially dependent on just exactly how the agenda of the questions under consideration happens to be constituted. And if a question does *not* figure in the agenda of explicitly entertained issues ('Is the Vegetarian candidate acceptable?') then there simply is no disagreement about it.

The salient point is that consensus/dissensus relates not to inferrable commonalities but to how we do or would answer the questions that actually arise in the cognitive context at issue. Consensus, then, has to be construed in terms of addressing common issues in a common way. But how does such consilience bear on the issue of truth?

3.2 *Truth, Objectivity, and Consensus*

Given that 'the truth is one', we can endorse without question the idea that in so far as people arrive at the truth, they will agree with one another, that is, will enter into consensus. But of course this (unproblematic) approach hitches consensus to the wagon of truth. The challenging question is: can one proceed in reverse, can one somehow hitch truth to the wagon of consensus? Considering that 'the truth' as such seems to be something absolute and transcendent while consensus is something more mundane and accessible, various philosophers have dreamt of the prospect of going for consensus and letting truth look after itself. Unfortunately, however, it would seem that in epistemology as in social life there is no such thing as a free lunch. The appeal of a consensus approach to truth is easy to understand. But its workability is something else again.

Some theorists—J. S. Mill and Jürgen Habermas for example—think that truly open and unrestrained (non-constrained, unrepressed) dialogue and discussion is virtually bound to lead to an ultimate agreement on the truth of the matter. Such a doctrine has two problems. The first involves the somewhat utopian idea that a properly managed dialogue must—inexorably—issue ultimately in agreement rather than simply sharper and harder disagreement—as seems actually to happen much of the time in real life. The second, even more serious difficulty relates to the idea that consensus stands co-ordinate with truth: that where there is consensus there is truth and where there is truth it will ultimately enforce a consensus through its inherent attractions.

As Habermas sees it, rational discussion is an objectifying process because it must transpire in a language, and 'the selected speech-system will *ipso facto* decide what sorts of data can be introduced as evidence in a given context of argumentation, i.e. what sorts of backing are admissible'.[1] On such a view, 'the language' that discussants are supposed to share in common itself already provides a mechanism for settling issues of factual appropriateness. But this seems very unrealistic. For languages are the imperfect instruments of imperfect humans, and linguistic appropriateness of itself is no guarantor of truth. The appropriateness of our language use in speaking of a 'sunrise' or 'sunset' does not mean that the sun actually does any rising or setting. The 'objectivity' inherent in the individual-transcendent impersonality of language is nowise a hallmark of truth—it betokens no more than communicative efficacy within a given framework of opinion. Usage that is 'correct' in the sense of appropriateness need not be 'correct' in the sense of factuality.

The ensuing discussion will examine some major themes regarding the relationship between truth and consensus. It will argue that consensuality neither constitutes a conceptually

---

[1] Jürgen Habermas, *Vorstudien und Ergänzungen zur Theorie des kommunikativen Handelns* (Berlin, 1984), 166.

inherent part of the *definition* of truth, nor yet affords a workable *test-criterion* of truth. The most that can be supported along these general lines is that consensus can play the role of an *evidential* consideration—that in suitable circumstances the fact of its consensual endorsement can be taken to provide some modest degree of *evidential support* for a reasonable belief in the truth of a certain proposition. But of course a positive evidential factor is something that goes only a short distance; it is not something upon which—of and by itself—we can base any large and weighty claims.

Consider the idea that a consensual criterion of truth should play the role of an inductive principle regarding certain groups of believers, based on a sufficiently successful track record:

> When and if all (or most) people of the group S agree in accepting a certain contention as true, then it indeed is true.

This general line of approach to truth-determination could be implemented by constituting the group S either *descriptively* (Greeks, humans-in-general, scientists, doctors of philosophy) or *normatively* (competent people, sagacious experts). In the former case, however, the available facts are not very favourable towards the thesis under consideration—on all available indications, the performance of *descriptively* constituted groups is not all that impressive. (It is not easy to come away from even a casual look at the history of science—or indeed at intellectual history in general—with an unimpaired conviction that consensus is a touchstone of truth.) And in the latter case, the consensus-criteriology thesis verges on triviality in view of the apparently circular way of constituting the normative groups at issue (in the extreme case by taking them to consist of 'perfect cognitive agents'—or gods).[2] Either way, the

---

[2] Karl-Otto Apel does not help matters by telling us that our epistemic limitations mean that, following Peirce, we should treat consensus as the functional equivalent of divine judgement (as 'das für uns massgebende Äquivalent für die von uns nicht verfügbare Sicht Gottes'). ('Fallibilismus, Konsenstheorie der Wahrheit, und Letztbegründung', in H. Schnädelbach, *et al.* (eds.), *Philosophie und Begründung* (Frankfurt am Main, 1987), see p. 163.) This thesis shatters on our all too clear recognition that the principle, *vox populi, vox dei*, obtains in matters of inquiry no more than it does in those of politics. Like Peirce and Habermas before him, Apel rescues this position by recourse to an idealization that is not more accessible to us *de facto* than is the mind of God.

prospect of a consensus criteriology for truth determination is not a particularly promising one.

To be sure, it would be a mistake to invoke the cognitive limitations of consensus as a basis for scepticism by arguing as follows:

no consensus → no objective 'truth of the matter'

This position is predicated on the principle that 'if different people can (justifiedly) think differently about some issue, then there just is no objective fact of the matter with regard to it'. It takes the line of a nihilistic relativism which holds that where there is no rationally enforceable consensus, the issue just is not an objective one: there just is no 'fact of the matter', but only mere opinion—or arbitrary decision. This attribution of dire implications to unavailable consensus dates back to the teachings of the sceptics of classical antiquity. It emerged in the last of the ten *tropes*, or arguments for scepticism inventoried by Sextus Empiricus in his *Pyrrhonian Hypotypôses*.[3] This invoked the variation across the range of culturally diverse views in matters of custom, manners, laws, and (above all) beliefs to establish the infeasibility of our ever discovering the truth about such issues. Throughout the sceptical tradition, the variation of customs and beliefs has been invoked in this sort of way to support a deconstructionism that takes a lack of consensus to betoken an absence of the objective factuality needed for meaningful deliberation. The prospect of different constructions—different interpretations or opinions—is taken to annihilate the matters in view as objectively factual issues.

The vitiating flaw of the sceptical construal of dissensus is that it involves begging a pivotal question. For to validate a move from the datum 'People do not agree about *X*' to the conclusion '*X* does not represent a genuine issue of objective fact', what is required is clearly a mediating premiss to the following effect:

If *X* is an authentic factual issue, then rational people will, of necessity, come to reach agreement about it.

But the more closely one looks at this thesis, the less plausible it appears. Where is the Moses who has come down from the mountain with a stone-graven guarantee that whenever there

---

[3] See bk. 1, 145 ff.

indeed are facts, all right-minded inquirers will come to discern them with an accuracy that precludes disagreement? However plausible this view may be with regard to some rather simple-minded issues, it makes little sense to take the line that it holds across the board.

Sceptics through the ages have been wilfully blind to how little actually follows from a lack of consensus. For one thing, one cannot appropriately argue: 'Consensus *has not* been achieved; therefore, consensus *cannot* be achieved.' But more seriously yet, one cannot even argue: 'Consensus cannot be achieved, therefore, there is no truth or fact of the matter.' In the cognitive case, for example, there are clearly different defensible answers to questions like 'What sort of person was Napoleon?' or 'What motivated Caesar's decision to cross the Rubicon?' But de-objectification certainly does not follow— our inability to reach consensus in rational inquiry about such issues just does not entail that there is no sort of objective 'fact of the matter' at issue, and that any set of opinions is as good (or bad) as any other.

It is notorious that people disagree in eyewitness reports about the description of a perpetrator or about the size of a crowd in a public square. And different historical cultures have held very different views on the issue of whether the blood ebbs and flows in its channels or whether it circulates. We certainly do not expect the natural science of other eras— of our remote predecessors, say, or even of our eventual successors—to agree with ours. But the prospect (or even reality) of disagreement does not prevent such issues from being objective matters of correct and incorrect assertion. (And there is no good reason to think the situation to be all that different with respect to social or political matters where we are prepared to face disagreement with comparative equanimity.) The existence of dissensus within it does not imply the subjectivity of a rational enterprise.

After all, we can readily account for a failure of consensus in ways that do not at all countervail against the existence of facts of the matter. In the case of factual information, for example, the circumstance of *evidential* diversity—obtaining because different people have different bodies of evidence at their disposal—makes for a differentiation of belief that is perfectly warranted, and indeed rationally mandated. And in the case of evaluation, the circumstance of *experiential* diversity (the fact that different people have different bodies of experience at their disposal) makes for a natural differentiation of appraisal that is perfectly warranted, and indeed rationally mandated. And much the same holds for our practical judgements about the appropriateness of actions. In no case need dissensus betoken an absence of rational cogency.

There is, however, one important aspect of consensual agreement that does need to be considered, namely that relating to the sort of attitude that rational people will take towards the consensuality of what they believe to be true. The principle, 'no consensus → no truth', is by contraposition logically equivalent to: 'truth → consensus'. That is, it amounts to the idea that where there indeed is a truth of the matter, a consensus about it will eventually emerge. But does this make sense—does truth require consensuality?

Consider the following sequence of theses: *A rational person will accept a contention* p *(as true) only if he or she believes that*:

1. Every other person also accepts *p*.
2. Every other *rational* person also accepts *p*.
3. Every other rational person *would* also accept *p* if placed in the same epistemic circumstances.

Here (1) is clearly untenable: it wears its own absurdity on its sleeve; it makes no sense to limit one's beliefs to only three things that *everyone* endorses. And (2) is also implausible, among other reasons because we cannot expect people (even if fully rational) to accept a truth if all the evidence at their disposal points the other way. Only (3) maintains a plausible linkage of consensuality to rational belief. But (3) has a rather special sort of status. For it obtains simply because it is incumbent on rational people to take this stance towards something they believe to be true: what is at issue is ultimately not a fact about the relation of consensus as such to truth, but rather a fact about the nature of rational belief. When Habermas claims that rational consensus is the ultimate criterion of truth, the kindest, most favourable way to interpret this is as making a claim not so much about the nature of truth as about the nature of an (idealized) rational consensus.

Consensus, after all, is a matter of the substance of people's views and hinges crucially on such variable matters as evidence, methodological commitments, and 'climate of opinion'. Consensus in the community of inquirers, is a matter of *how people think* about things on the basis of the evidence at their disposal. And in a complex world such consilience of data is more than we can generally expect. It is clearly problematic to contend that whenever there is a fact of the matter, people are bound to acquire enough of the right sort of evidence to find it out.

The sceptical inference 'no consensus, therefore no objective factuality' is deeply flawed. To insist on consensus as such is to maintain that in the *actual* circumstance people *will* reach agreement with respect to the issues. To insist on objectivity is to maintain that in ideal circumstances people *would* reach agreement. And these are very different matters.[4] Difficulties in achieving consensus emphatically do not preclude objectivity. Consensus turns on what people think; objectivity on what is actually so. To see dissensus as annihilating objective factuality is to blame reality for our own cognitive limitations and imperfections. It is the epistemic equivalent of Aesop's story of the Fox and the Grapes.

No doubt, substantial disagreement on the issues will (and should) engender caution, undermining any facile confidence that we have actually got it right. But there are no adequate grounds for construing disagreement—even stubbornly enduring disagreement—to mean that there just is no objective fact to disagree about. In various areas of perfectly meaningful inquiry and deliberation we not only presently lack consensus but, as best we can tell, may never achieve it.

But is 'the scientific method' not by its very nature a guarantor of consensus? Certainly not in any realistic mode. We have an idealized vision of the scientific process in terms of 'comprehensively complete information, processed with perfect

---

[4] On the other hand, it is conceivable that even the step to idealization might not produce consensus. For where there are 'different sorts of ideals'—where various principles might be at odds with one another even in circumstances of idealization—people need not come to agreement. Even 'ideally rational agents' working under 'ideally favourable conditions' might nevertheless give different priorities and emphases to various sorts of cognitive positivities (uniformity, say, and simplicity).

adequacy', and accordingly look to the production of a fixed single result in which all rational inquirers will agree—a consensus of the cognitively competent. But in projecting such a rational consensuality in the cognitive domain, we lose sight of how unrealistic this practise is. In matters of inquiry there is no natural compulsion that of necessity impels all competent minds to a uniform result. In theoretical no less than in practical matters, different backgrounds of experience can, quite cogently, lead different (otherwise competent) investigations to entirely different evaluations of the one selfsame situation. After all, even in matters of purely formal science we do not face a situation of consensuality. In logic both classical and non-classical systems find their exponents who take rather different views of valid inference. In mathematics too we have both classical and intuitionistic theorists, constructionistic and conjecturalistic schools of thought. Everywhere we look about us, we see variety and dissensus. Those who cannot come to terms with conflict seemingly can find no secure refuge in this real world of ours.

Consider, in particular, the situation in the natural sciences. However much consensus may exist in this domain at any one particular time, there is certainly no transtemporal agreement—no diachronic consensus. The history of science is a story of changes of mind. Where are the agreed 'scientific truths' of yester-year—the humours of Galen, the absolute space of the Newtonian era, the luminiferous ether of turn-of-the-century physics? And there is no good reason to think this process will come to a stop. The scientists of the year 3,000 will think our presently accepted theories every bit as inadequate as we deem those of our predecessors of 300 years ago. There is no reason to think that progress will ever come to a stop in a definitive 'final resolution', a definitive consensus enduring henceforward across the generations. (But, of course, this is no ground for seeing science as a futile enterprise preoccupied with looking for answers in a sphere where there simply are no objective facts.)

Consensus is thus no highway to truth—and no substitute for an objective criteriology. But it does, in one way, afford a useful epistemic instrumentality. For once we possess objectively cogent standards for the determination of competence—

for the identification of those who have a good track record at providing us with plausible indications of 'the truth of the matter'—then we can resort to the idea of a *consensus of the competent* to guide us in our decision regarding the rational acceptability of contentions. Consensus can thus provide an instrumentality of *plausible estimation*, albeit only in situations where cogent—and thus more than *merely* consensual—standards are in hand. However, this recognition of the epistemological–criteriological utility of consensus is clearly something very different from the position of a thesis that sees consensus as providing a functional equivalent of truth—let alone as constituting its essence. Consensus can be invoked to *extend* the range of what is rationally acceptable as true, but it cannot be invoked to *delineate* this range.

3.3 *Ideality and Consensus*

We have to come to terms with two facts, neither of which can simply be dismissed: (1) in matters of importance in the cognitive and evaluative domains it is generally impossible to achieve a pervasive consensus, and (2) unless a factual or evaluative claim stakes a claim to universal validity (unless it makes an *Anspruch auf Universalität*) it does not really qualify as a claim to the authentically true, or good, or right (etc.). And the reconciliation of these considerations proceeds along roughly Kantian lines. The staking of claims ('*p* is true'; '*X* is good') stands in the order of actuality, where consensus may well fail us. The claim to universality, by contrast, stands in the normative (let us avoid *noumenal*!) order, and pivots on how things *ought* to go—how they stand not in the real but in the ideal order of things. In sum, the consensuality so dear to Habermas, Apel, and their congeners can at best and at most be regarded as a matter of idealization.

The emphasis of consensus theorists like Jürgen Habermas and Karl Otto Apel upon an 'ideal speech situation' is thus easy to understand.[5] For the epistemic realities are such that

---

[5] Regarding Apel's position, see especially his long essay in 'Fallibilismus, Konsenztheorie der Wahrheit, und Letztbegründung', in W. R. Köhler, *et al.* (eds.), *Philosophie und Begründung* (Frankfurt am Main, 1987).

consensus among rational inquirers across the divides of time and culture is not something that often (let alone necessarily) happens in the real world. The fact is that the link of consensus to objective factuality seems plausible at the level of idealization—only perfectly competent and totally well-informed inquirers can be expected to reach a consensus on factual matters.

To say that truth and correctness should be able to make good their claims on the agreement of people (*'dass die Wahrheit und Richtigkeit diskursiv einlösbare Geltungsansprüche sind'*, as Habermas puts it[6]) sounds well and good. But the truth in matters of scientific complexity can in fact be made evidentially secure only in ideal circumstances, and not in general under the imperfect conditions in which we humans actually conduct our cognitive affairs—now or ever. The truth as such will compel agreement in and of itself only from those whose epistemic situation is suitably favourable. In this imperfect sublunary dispensation, consensus is too much to expect—or to ask for, given the variation of experience among intelligent beings. We are committed to the universality and objectivity of rational judgements because we see such judgements as implementing universal principles. But consensuality is not something we should demand here and now. Truth and consensus converge only in the ideal limit—only when we can contemplate the sort of agreement that would be reached by ideally rational inquiries working under ideally favourable conditions.

And of course this sort of idealization carries us well outside the range of the 'practical politics' of humanity's conduct of its cognitive affairs. An ideal inquiry as such has to be construed as one where:

1. The inquirers are 'ideally rational' in that they use all and only the appropriate (correct, valid) procedures, methods, techniques, and do so in an optimal way, and,
2. There are no limitations on resources: the inquirers have at their disposal 'everything they need' to operate within the limits of the possible, lacking no time, energy, observational or computational power, etc.

[6] Habermas, *Vorstudien und Ergänzungen zur Theorie des kommunikativen Handelns* (Frankfurt am Main, 1984), 159.

It does not take much imagination to realize that this sort of idealization removes the discussion from the operational range of the effective criteriology of human inquiry.[7]

Above, we considered (and rejected) the implication from truth to consensuality. Let us now look at the reverse implication from consensuality to truth. Consider the following sequence of theses, implementing the idea of consensus as a criterion of truth:

(1)   If everyone maintains p, then p
(2)   If everyone who is fully rational maintains p, then p
(3)   If everyone who is fully rational and who is placed in ideally benign epistemic circumstances maintains p, then p

As regards (1), it is clear that the idea that consensus is an index of truth shatters on the epistemic frailty and fallibility of *homo sapiens*—on the real-world impact of fashions, bandwagons, and the idols of the tribe. Even rational people stand subject to the limitations of their time and place, so that (2) is in difficulty as well. It emerges that only (3) is appropriate. But its appropriateness is, in the final analysis, not something that pivots on consensuality as such. For a good case can be made out for maintaining that even the following singular thesis is true:

(3*)   If *anyone* (i.e. any particular individual) who is fully rational and who is placed in ideally benign epistemic circumstances maintains p then p

In the final analysis, the thesis has nothing to do with consensuality as such. The criteriological 'consensus theory of truth' with respect to the ideal case is not something that actually turns on the nature of consensus, but rather on our idea of what 'ideal rationality' is all about (namely that in 'identical circumstances' it will transpire that 'ideally rational' agents will proceed in the same way). But it is rationality and

---

[7] Thus when Apel insists that 'it is necessary in rational argumentation to presuppose methodologically that error in a psychological sense (such as mistakes in calculation) can be excluded' ('Fallibilismus', 173), he does not reckon with the ominous consequences of this view. Whenever one prescinds from errors of reasoning as 'merely psychological' one implicitly acknowledges the irrelevancy of one's theory to human affairs. Realistically speaking, it lies in the nature of human fallibility that a consensus is in principle no less fallible than any personal opinion.

not consensus that is doing the work for us here. What matters for rationality is not *that* people accept something in common, but *how* they come to do so—not consensuality as such but the process by which it comes about. (And it is exactly here that the factor of idealization must be introduced as a further item added *ab extra*.)

And so, what the careful scrutiny of theses (1)–(3) shows is that while linkage between truth and consensus indeed exists, it does so only at the level of a rather remote idealization. Accordingly, one would be ill advised to invoke consensuality as a *standard* (a deciding criterion) of truth, because the idealization needed to make consensuality meaningful automatically renders this supposed criterion deeply problematic.

When and where we find it, consensus, no doubt, is a pleasant thing to have. In its presence we can feel encouragingly reassured of being on the right track—although St Augustine's dictum *securus iudicat orbis terrarum* doubtless overstates the matter. But consensus is not something on which we should insist so strongly that we should feel at a loss in the presence of issues that lack the benefit of its reassuring presence.

After all, even where consensus exists, it may not be meaningful: the agreement at issue may be no more than an agreement in folly. Clearly, people can agree on incorrect beliefs and on inappropriate (or counter-productive) values or courses of action. Consensus just is not an unqualified good; it is something one has to evaluate. It is only a good thing when what is at issue is a consensus in what is actually true, right, just, and the like. In and of itself—without reference to its object—consensus is a neutral, value-indeterminate condition, analogous, in this regard, to such things as *dedication* to a cause or *personal conviction* in a belief. Consensus as such, is not automatically positive.

It is clearly not all that hard to produce concrete examples of how consensus can be counter-productive. In scientific inquiry, for example, there are many situations in which the best interests of effective progress will be served by 'mixed strategies' of inquiry, with different investigators (or groups) pursuing different lines of investigation in an endeavour to solve a certain problem. Many problems are most effectively handled when different lines of inquiry are pursued by investigators who are committed to different theories and hold different opinions on the relevant questions.[8] The best interests of problem-solving overall are often served by a 'division of labour' among rival individuals or groups whose positions on the issues are competing and conflicting.

3.4 *The Consensus Theory of Truth*

Jürgen Habermas has claimed: 'I can [correctly] ascribe a predicate to an object if and only if every person who could enter into a dialogue with me *would* ascribe the same predicate to the same object. . . . The condition of the truth of statements is the potential agreement of all others.'[9] The crucial question here, of course, is exactly who these 'all others' are and under what conditions they would agree. Clearly they will not be real people of flesh and blood; they can only be ideally rational agents proceeding in ideally favourable epistemic conditions. For otherwise any claim of this sort is patently untenable.

What then are we to make of the 'consensus theory of truth'? Let us contemplate the linkage of truth to consensus in its *temporal* aspect. Consider the following series of (increasingly weakened) theses:

(1) p is indeed true → a consensus regulating p's truth *has been reached*

(2) p is indeed true → a consensus regarding p's truth *will (eventually) be reached*

(3) p is indeed true → a consensus regarding p's truth *can be reached*

(4) p is indeed true → a consensus regarding p's truth *would be reached* if ideal conditions prevailed

Here (1) is simply untenable, owing to the megalomania of its implied claim that the currently existing community is

---

[8] A cogent case for this position has been articulated by Husain Sarkar, 'A Theory of Group Rationality', *Studies in History and Philosophy of Science*, 13 (1982), 55–72. Cf. also ch. 5 of his book, *A Theory of Method* (Berkeley, Calif., 1983).

[9] 'Wahrheitstheorien', in H. Fahrenbach (ed.), *Wirklichkeit und Reflexion: Festschrift für Walter Schulz* (Pfüllingen, 1973), 219.

omniscient. Thesis (2) is C. S. Peirce's position of inquiry's ultimate (asymptotic) realization of the real truth of things—a millenarian theory that has few visible means of support. Thus (3) and (4) are the only safe bets. But this circumstance does no more than establish a linkage that is, alas, so weak as not to be very interesting. We live in a world of recalcitrant realities, not in a realm of abstract possibilities and theoretical ideals.

On the other hand, consider the converse series:

(5)   The consensus among inquirers is in p's favour → p is indeed true

(6)   The consensus among inquirers will (eventually) be in p's favour → p is indeed true

(7)   The consensus among inquirers can be in p's favour → p is indeed true

(8)   Epistemically ideal conditions prevail and a consensus in p's favour exists → p is indeed true

Here (5) is counter-indicated by a vast array of historical evidence. Moreover, the idea that what is currently agreed upon nowadays is indeed true imputes a capacity to our contemporaries which few sensible people would seriously endorse. Thesis (6) carries us back to yet another aspect of the deeply problematic Peircean idea of cognitive millenarianism—of the flawlessness of an eventually emergent community of inquirers. And thesis (7) flies in the face of the ease with which we can envision scenarios that have people coming to communal agreement on blatant errors. Only (8) is a safe bet. And this points once more to the significant conclusion that the linkage of consensus to truth is strictly a matter of idealization.

Again, consider the following sequence of theses:

(1)   If p, then everyone *does* maintain (realize, agree) that p

(2)   If p, then everyone who is fully rational *does* maintain that p

(3)   If p, then everyone who is fully rational *should* maintain that p (and would do so if ideal circumstances obtained)

It is pretty clear that (1) is simply false: people just are not omniscient. Nor is (2) all that plausible, since even a fully rational person could surely not be expected to maintain something—even something that is in fact true—when all the evidence at hand points the other way. Clearly, the most that can be said along these general lines is (3) with its indispensible recourse to idealization. The sort of position at issue can only be upheld in doubly ideal circumstances: it can only stipulate what *'perfectly rational'* people would realize about true facts in *'ideally benign'* epistemic circumstances. (This consideration alone shows that it makes little sense to regard consensus as part of the *definition* of truth since the idealization involved clearly begs the issue.)

But even if one joins Habermas in viewing consensus as a cognitively regulative ideal, one must realize that this has few—if any—practical implications. In particular, it would by no means follow from this that steps leading towards consensus are necessarily progressive and steps away from it necessarily regressive in relation to the cognitive stake at issue. For we must recognize the fallaciousness of the idea that when one would ideally like to have X (globally), every individual step towards X (locally) is thereby positive and productive on grounds of 'leading us towards X's realization'. Frequently one must undertake temporary deviations away from one's favoured goal in order actually to get closer to it (as when travelling through the Panama Canal). If any and every move towards consensus were for that reason productive, we would be well advised to make our own opinions give way to those of other people—a policy which all too clearly leads not towards truth but simply towards the triumph of the stubborn.

It is important to stress in this context that to downgrade consensus-seeking as an epistemic resource is by no means to reject the value of cognitive interaction with others by way of discussion, controversy, information pooling, and probing for the roots of disagreement. Anything that expands our informational horizons clearly enhances the epistemic basis of our beliefs. But what validates these communal processes in inquiry is not a preconception that reaching consensus is the governing goal; it is only the consideration that in the epistemic and evidential domain bigger is better—that more amply evidentiated conclusions are for that very reason better substantiated, and that taking the beliefs of others into account is one way to broaden our evidential basis.

To reiterate the previous concession, consensus can serve as a positive evidential factor. However, any theorist who, like Peirce or Habermas, regards consensus as an index of truth must provide an explanatory rationale for how it is that consensus can bear the burden of truth-indicativeness. For the transition from consensuality to truth—or the reverse—is by no means obvious or automatic. Unrealistic idealization aside, it is, on all available tellings, very far from plausible to co-ordinate truth and consensus. Considerations of abstract general principle ('conceptual considerations') lead to truth only from *ideal* consensus (when 'perfectly rational inquirers' proceed on the basis of a 'perfected body of data'). The very most that an *actual* consensus can do for us is to afford *some* evidence (and in general distinctly *weak* evidence) that an ideal consensus can be assumed or expected.

In the practical business of inquiry we do not have a royal road to the truth as such. Rather, the rocky road of *estimation based on imperfect data* is generally the best and most that we can manage. And here consensus exerts its appeal as an evidential factor of undoubted (albeit very limited) authority. But between this point and a 'consensus theory of truth' there lies a vast and ultimately unbridgeable gulf.

The injunction 'Find out the consensus opinion!' is much like the injunction 'Look it up in the encyclopaedia!' Following its dictates may be, by and large, a useful and practicable way at our disposal for forming a plausible judgement about where 'the truth of the matter' lies. For those not expert on the issues, it may be the most sensible way to proceed. (After all, we cannot telephone to the Recording Angel and ask!) But it has no logical bearing on the nature of 'the truth', and plays no decisive role in its rational criteriology. Even where consensus exists we are well advised to take it with a grain of salt. If consensus were a guarantor of truth we would feel very differently about it than we actually do. Sensible people presumably do not deem themselves entitled to take a potentially highly dangerous course of action (releasing a conceivably virulent germ into the atmosphere, say) simply because a consensus exists that it is safe. We can plausibly view consensus as a basis for warranted confidence but clearly not as a guarantor of truth.

Certainly as far as the outsiders of a given discipline are concerned, the consensus of its expert practitioners (physicians, say, or nuclear physicists) on some issue in this field should be seen as a decisive probative consideration in its favour. Moreover, when other things are anything like equal with respect to p, then it is plausible to suppose that:

pr (p/people agree that p) > pr (p/people disagree concerning p)

The reason for this is not far to seek. Agreement is indicative of an *invariance* of sorts: it reflects the face that, not withstanding the variation of the particular epistemic stance of different individuals, people's efforts at epistemic problem-solving favour one particular outcome. And this sort of invariance is clearly a positive evidential factor. A 'consensus theory of reasonable belief' along such lines accordingly has something to be said in its favour. But the step from reasonable belief to truth is neither easy nor unproblematic. The link between consensuality and truth is so weak that it is unpromising to project a 'consensus theory of truth' in any meaningful sense of the term. The purely *evidential* relation just considered it certainly no basis for this; one might as soon contemplate a 'theory of truth' based on the idea that *in vino veritas*.

It is only realism—and not disloyalty to the truth—to recognize that others, whose cognitive situation is different from ours, may regard as true what we ourselves see as error: that the advantages of the truth (whatever they are) are not of such a sort that they automatically appeal to inquirers, ir-respective of their epistemic position in the scheme of things: the particular course of their experiences, and their training, natural inclination, etc. There is thus no sound reason whatsoever why our own dedication to the truth and our own commitment to the quest for its attainment should be diminished by a recognition of the circumstance that others may resolve the issues differently and see matters differently from ourselves.

In his classic essay *On Liberty*, J. S. Mill spells out with vivid clarity the dangers of an insistence on consensus and conformity. Unless people are left to their own dissonant devices, progress is impeded, the search for truth hampered, the free development of personalities stunted. The weight of 'collative mediocrity' will crush all impetus to originality, inventiveness, and creativity.

No disloyalty to the truth is involved in accepting the reality—and understandability—of the circumstance that, do what we will in matters of rational inquiry, we may nevertheless not be able to get other people to see things our way. An insistence upon the achievement of consensus just is not an instrument indispensable to the pursuit of truth—an enterprise that can and does exist and flourish in the absence of consensus. The prospect of dissensus does not show that the pursuit of truth is futile, but merely that it is—like so much else in life—complex, difficult, and controversial.

3.5 A Contrast Case

It is instructive to contrast Habermas's approach to consensus with that of Richard Rorty. From Habermas's point of view, consensus is a powerful instrument because, properly constituted, it provides for the rational solutions to problems. Consensuality thus affords a royal road to rationality. By contrast, Rorty, in the manner of the ancient sophists,[10] takes consensus as providing, not a way towards rationality, but a *substitute* for it.

As Rorty sees it, there is no prospect of any sort of objective validation of claims to the actual *truth* of beliefs or the *adequacy* of methods. All we have is *consensus*: an agreement in the community to address issues in a certain sort of way:

Dewey and Foucault [i.e. right-minded philosophers] . . . agree, right down the line, with the need to abandon traditional notions of rationality, objectivity, method, and truth. . . . They agree that rationality is what history and society make it—that there is no overarching historical structure (the Value of Man, the laws of human nature, the Moral Law, the Nature of Society) to be discovered.[11]

[10] Cf. ch. 1 sect. 1.3 above.
[11] Richard Rorty, *Consequences of Pragmatism* (Minneapolis, 1982), 204.

The traditional rational fixities now crumble away, and all we have left to guide us in the conduct of the life of the mind—in understanding and evaluation—are the customs of the tribe, the practice of the community, the contingencies of history and society. Consensus is king not because it provides a royal road to rationality, but because, classical rationality having vanished, consensus is simply all we have left to cling to.

That is, if and when we have it. For why should consensus ever come into being at all? If 'rationality is whatever history and society make it' why should there be any such 'rationality'-defining consensus at all instead of chaos and confusion? If people and societies have no inherent nature—no common make-up, no common interests, no common problems and solutions—then how can a stable consensus ever spring into being (save by some totally fortuitous gift of the gods that we have no reason to expect)? If there are genuinely no commonalities, then how can people ever configure the sort of history and society needed to constitute even a merely consensual rationality? A salient difficulty with Rorty's objectivity-abandoning approach is that it substitutes for a uniformity of nature the social glue of an artefactual uniformity which—in the circumstances—there is no reason for expecting, and no basis for explaining if and when it should happen to arise.

Habermas's 'rationality via consensus' approach is predicated upon very unrealistic expectations of consensus—namely, that it should provide a means towards something akin to rationality as traditionally conceived. On the other hand, Rorty's 'let's just abandon "human nature"' approach leaves us with a consensuality which—if and when we find it—is no more than an empty shell, a pointless *coincidence* in both senses of that term. Neither theory provides us with a conception of consensus capable of accomplishing any constructive work.

4

The Experiential Basis of Cognitive Diversity and the Unavoidability of Pluralism

4.1 *Rational Judgement and Experience*

To acquiesce in a diversity of opinions—to tolerate dissensus—is to accept pluralism.[1] However, deliberations about cognitive pluralism will have to confront the question of just what it is that one is going to be a pluralist about. Is it to be a pluralism of *beliefs* or a pluralism of *methods*—of cognitive commitments or of cognitive procedures, processes, and standards?

Clearly, method pluralism is something stronger than belief pluralism. Given the generality and power of what is at issue in a *method*, with its inherent multiplicity of applications, it follows that when authentically different cognitive methods are at work, then at least some of the resultant beliefs are bound to be different as well. And conversely, a consensus of beliefs across the entire range would indicate that there is consensus on methods as well. For where the beliefs at issue agree altogether, then there will be no justificatory basis for any differentiation with regard to these methods that we employ in resolving cognitive issues.

But the reverse does not hold: different beliefs do not necessarily involve different methods. Even when the cognitive

[1] Until the early years of the 20th c., 'pluralism' designated the metaphysical doctrine of a variety of diverse *substances*—of things or types of thing. Only as the century progressed did a different sense come to prominence: the epistemological doctrine of a variety of diverse positions, all viewed as being more or less appropriate and plausible.

methods are the same, the same beliefs need not result, since, for example, the one selfsame scientific-inductive method will, when oriented towards different bodies of accepted data, quite appropriately yield very different results. Belief dissensus accordingly does not carry method dissensus in its wake.[2]

The present discussion of cognitive pluralism will accordingly focus on beliefs rather than methods—primarily for two reasons: (1) Since method pluralism entails belief pluralism, the implications of the latter would follow from the former as well; (2) Since the present deliberations are predicated on a definite particular notion of rationality—one which envisions the standard scientific-inductive method as having a position of primacy in matters of cognition and inquiry regarding the world's ways—the issue of method pluralism becomes moot. For the fact is that even this single optimally rational method—the scientific-inductive—is not only compatible with the prospect of a cognitive pluralism but actually invites its acceptance.

People conduct their problem-solving affairs on the basis of weaving new information into the fabric of the old. They construe the implications of new data in the light of their background information. Someone complains of feeling unwell. The person whose friends are all hypochondriacs thinks nothing of it. The person whose friends are all bursting with vigour and good health draws the direst conclusions. That selfsame datum plays a substantially different informative role in different contexts. Conforming or deviating from a pre-established pattern of normalcy makes all the difference in how a given piece of information is to be interpreted. A differential background of experience plausibly enough leads different people into disagreement.

Rational inquiry is a matter of aligning our views with the substance of our experience. It calls for making judgements that achieve the most harmonious overall co-ordination between the information afforded us by our experience and our question-answering endeavours. Its products are thus not

---

[2] The point at issue in these observations is grasped rather more easily in symbolic than in verbal formulation. It is that we accept '= beliefs $\rightarrow$ = methods', or equivalently: '$\neq$ methods $\rightarrow$ $\neq$ beliefs'. But we reject the converse '$\neq$ beliefs $\rightarrow$ $\neq$ methods', or equivalently: '= methods $\rightarrow$ = beliefs'.

the perfected deliverances of an impersonal world spirit, but the laboriously constructed makeshift contrived by imperfect humans in the course of an active engagement in the world's affairs—an ongoing interaction between inquirer and environment. They do not issue from intersubjectively invariant factors, but emerge from the reactions of individual agents proceeding on the basis of their personalized—though not necessarily idiosyncratic—backgrounds of experience.[3] The 'facts' they purport inhere in personally conditioned reactions to prevailing circumstances, a state of affairs that helps to explain why even rigorously rationalistic investigators often resort to assertions about what they 'find it difficult to accept' or 'cannot bring myself to believe'. (This prominent role of personal experience and individual reaction in the rational validation of ideas also helps to account for philosophers' perennial complaints about being misunderstood.)

The solutions we adopt to resolve our questions about the world are the products of evidentially substantiated conjectures. Scientific theorizing in particular is a matter of an inductive triangulation from observations—of question-resolving conjecture inductively projected from the data of experience. And (sensibly enough) our ventures into inductive inference involve the construction of the most economical cognitive structures to house these data comfortably. Inductive reasoning seeks out the simplest overall patterns of regularity that can adequately accommodate the available information regarding cases-in-hand, and then projects them across the entire spectrum of possibilities in order to answer our general questions. Be it in science or in everyday life, the rational formation of opinion rests on fundamentally inductive processes that involve the search for, or construction of, the least complex belief-structure capable at once of answering our questions and accommodating the available data.

This issue of 'the available data' is crucial here. And this is clearly a contextually variable factor. For the 'phenomena' at our experiential disposal obviously depend not only on our exposure to nature's doings, but also on the changeable

---

[3] See the author's *Empirical Inquiry* (Oxford, 1982). Cf. also Michael Polanyi, *Personal Knowledge* (Chicago, 1974).

physical and conceptual instruments that we make use of when probing nature. Since we can only learn about nature by interacting with it, everything will depend on just where and how we bump up against nature in situations of observational and detectional interaction.

And what holds of science holds elsewhere as well. Rational inquirers attune their beliefs, expectations, and evaluations to the course of experience. It is, after all, the course of our experience with this world that determines what it is that is important and what is incidental, what is central and what is peripheral, what is normal and what is aberrant. Our basic assessments and expectations regarding the nature of things emerge from the patterns of our cognitive interactions with the world about us. The cognitive stance that people have is inevitably conditioned by the experiential flow of their interactions with reality. And experience is something that is bound to differ from age to age, culture to culture, and even— to some extent—from person to person. On this basis it becomes clear that a pluralism of cognitive commitments is an unavoidable part of the natural scheme of things. In sum, even when one particular method is at issue—the 'inductive' method of empirical inquiry—the experiential situation of its practitioner can and must engender a pluralism of substantially different results.

4.2 *Different Experiential Modes and the Prospect of Scientific Diversity*

Different social, temporal, and historical contexts equip different inquirers with different experiential resources. And this will, in the end, equip them with very different cognitive products as well.

To bring this point home in a particularly vivid way, let us consider the following question: 'To what extent would the natural science built up by the inquiring intelligences of an astronomically remote civilization be bound to resemble our own natural science?' In reflecting on this question and its ramifications, one soon comes to realize that there is an enormous potential for diversity.

Science is always the result of *inquiry* into nature, and this is inevitably a matter of a transaction or interaction in which nature is but one party and the inquiring beings another. On the basis of an *interactionist* model, there is no reason to think that the sciences of different civilizations will exhibit any significant resemblance to ours. It need not seem important to us—or, for that matter, even comprehensible. For we must expect that alien beings—if they exist—will be involved with nature in ways very different from our own.

A comparison of the 'science' of different civilizations here on earth suggests that it is not an outlandish hypothesis to suppose that the very *topics* of alien science might differ dramatically from those of our own. In our own case, for example, the fact that we live on the surface of the earth (unlike whales), the fact that we have eyes (unlike worms) and thus can *see* the heavens, the fact that we are so situated that the seasonal positions of heavenly bodies are intricately connected with a life-sustaining agriculture—all these factors are clearly connected with the development of astronomy. If those astronomically distant creatures experience nature in ways very different from ourselves, then they must obviously be expected to raise very different sorts of question. And, the mode of emplacement within nature of alien inquirers might be so different as to focus their attention on entirely different aspects or constituents of the cosmos. If the world is sufficiently complex and multifaceted, they might concentrate upon aspects of their environment that mean nothing to us, with the result that their natural science is oriented in directions very different from ours.[4]

The interests of creatures shaped under the remorseless pressure of evolutionary adaptations to very different—and endlessly variable—environmental conditions might well be oriented in directions very different from anything that is familiar to us.

---

[4] His anthropological investigations pointed Benjamin Lee Whorf in much this same direction. He wrote: 'The real question is: What do different languages do, not with artificially isolated objects, but with the flowing face of nature in its motion, color, and changing form; with clouds, beaches, and yonder flight of birds? For as goes our segmentation of the face of nature, so goes our physics of the cosmos' ('Language and Logic', in *Language, Thought, and Reality*, ed. J. B. Carroll (Cambridge, Mass., 1956), 240–1).

Laws are discernible regularities in nature. But discernment and detection will of course vary drastically with the mode of observation—that is, with the sort of resources that different creatures have at their disposal to do their detecting. Everything depends on how nature pushes back on our senses and their instrumental extensions. Even if we detect everything that we can, given our interests and sensibilities, we will not have got hold of everything available to others. And the converse is equally true. The laws that we (or anybody else) manage to formulate will depend crucially on our place within nature—on how we are connected into its wiring diagram, so to speak.

Again, alien intelligences might well scan nature very differently. Electromagnetic phenomena might lie altogether outside the ken of alien life-forms; if their environment does not afford them lodestones and electrical storms, the occasion to develop electromagnetic theory might never arise. The course of scientific development tends to flow in the channel of practical interests. A society of porpoises might well lack crystallography but develop a very sophisticated hydrodynamics; one comprised of mole-like creatures might never dream of developing optics or astronomy. One's language and thought processes are bound to be closely geared to the world as one experiences it. As is illustrated by the difficulties we ourselves experience in bringing the language of everyday experience to bear on subatomic phenomena, our concepts are ill attuned to facets of nature different in scale or structure from our own. We can hardly expect a 'science' that reflects such parochial preoccupations to be a universal fixture.

Most fundamentally, the *conceptualization* of an alien science might be very different from ours. For we must reckon with the possibility that a remote civilization might operate with a drastically different system of concepts in its cognitive dealings with nature. Different cultures and different intellectual traditions, to say nothing of different sorts of creature, are bound to describe and explain their experience—their world as they conceive it—in terms of concepts and categories of understanding substantially different from ours. They would diverge radically with respect to what the Germans call their *Denkmittel*—the conceptual instruments they employ in thought about the facts (or purported facts) of the world. They could, accordingly, be said to operate with different conceptual schemes, with different conceptual tools used to 'make sense' of experience—to characterize, describe, and explain the items that figure in the world as they view it. The taxonomic and explanatory mechanisms by means of which their cognitive business is transacted might differ so radically from ours that any intellectual contact with them would be difficult or impossible.

To insist on the monolithic uniqueness of science is to succumb to 'the myth of the God's eye-view'. Supporting considerations for this position have been advanced from very different points of departure. One example is a *Gedankenexperiment* suggested by Georg Simmel in the last century, which envisaged an entirely different sort of cognitive being—intelligent and actively inquiring creatures (animals, say, or beings from outer space) whose experiential modes are quite different from our own.[5] Their senses respond rather differently to physical influences: they are relatively insensitive, say, to heat and light, but highly sensitized to various electromagnetic phenomena. Such intelligent creatures, Simmel held, could plausibly be supposed to operate within a substantially different framework of empirical concepts and categories; the events and objects of the world of their experience might be very different from those of our own: their phenomenological predicates, for example, might have altogether variant descriptive domains. In a similar vein, William James wrote:

Were we lobsters, or bees, it might be that our organization would have led to our using quite different modes from these [actual ones of ours] of apprehending our experiences. It *might* be too (we cannot dogmatically deny this) that such categories unimaginable by us today, would have proved on the whole as serviceable for handling our experiences mentally as those we actually use.[6]

The science of a different civilization would inevitably be closely tied to the particular pattern of their interaction with nature as funnelled through the particular course of their

---

[5] Georg Simmel, 'Über eine Beziehung der Selektionslehre zur Erkenntnistheorie', *Archiv für systematische Philosophie und Soziologie*, 1 (1895), 34–45; see esp. 40–1.

[6] William James, *Pragmatism* (New York, 1907).

evolutionary adjustment to their specific environment. The 'forms of sensibility' of radically different beings (to invoke Kant's useful idea) are likely to be radically different from ours. The direct chemical analysis of environmental materials might prove highly useful, and bioanalytic techniques akin to our senses of taste and smell could be very highly developed, providing them with environmentally oriented 'experiences' of a very different sort.

The constitution of the alien inquirers—physical, biological, and social—thus emerges as crucial for science. It is bound to condition the agenda of questions and the instrumentalities for their resolution—to fix what is seen as interesting, important, relevant, and significant. Because of its pivotal role in determining what counts as an appropriate question and what is judged as an admissible solution, the cognitive posture of the inquirers must be expected to play a crucial role in shaping the course and character of scientific inquiry itself.

After all, throughout the earlier stages of man's intellectual history, different human civilizations developed their 'natural sciences' in ways substantially different from the situation we ourselves confront. And the shift to an extraterrestrial setting is bound to amplify this diversity enormously. The science of an alien civilization may be far more remote from ours than the language of our cousin the dolphin is remote from our language. Perhaps reluctantly, we must face the fact that on a cosmic scale the 'hard' physical sciences have something of the same cultural relativity that one encounters with the materials of the 'softer' social sciences on a terrestrial basis.

To clarify this idea of a conceptually different science, it helps to cast the issue in temporal rather than spatial terms. The descriptive characterization of *alien* science is a project somewhat analogous to that of describing our own *future* science. It is a key fact of life that progress in science is a process of *ideational* innovation that always places certain developments outside the intellectual horizons of earlier workers. The very concepts we think in terms of become available only in the course of scientific discovery itself. The science of remote aliens, as the science of the remote future, must be presumed to be such that we really could not achieve present intellectual access to it on the basis of our own current position in the cognitive scheme of things. Just as the technology of a more advanced civilization would be bound to strike us as magic, so its science would be bound to strike us an incomprehensible gibberish—until we had learned it 'from the ground up'. They might (just barely) be able to *teach* it to us, but they could not *explain* it to us by transposing it into our terms.

The most characteristic and significant difference between one conceptual scheme and another arises when the one scheme is committed to something that the other does not envisage at all—something lying entirely outside the conceptual range of the other. A typical case is that of the stance of Cicero's thought-world with regard to questions of quantum electrodynamics. The Romans of classical antiquity did not hold *different* views on these issues; they held no view at all about them. This whole set of relevant considerations remained outside their conceptual repertoire. The diversified history of *our* terrestrial science gives one some minuscule inkling of the vast range of possibilities along these lines.

The fundamental categories of reality-descriptive characterization that we standardly employ—the framework of spatiality and temporality, the ways and means of structural description, the linkages of functional connection, the causal mechanisms of explanatory rationalization, and the like—are not necessary features of intelligence as such. They are evolved cognitive adaptations to our own particular contingently constituted modes of emplacement in and interaction with nature—in short as historically developed products of our biological and cultural evolution. There is accordingly no reason to expect uniformity in this regard. Sociologists of knowledge tell us that even here on earth, our Western science is but one of many competing world-pictures. When one turns outward towards space at large, the prospects of diversity become literally endless. It is a highly problematic contention even that beings constituted as we are and located in an environment such as ours must inevitably describe and explain natural phenomena in our terms. And with differently constituted beings, the basis of differentiation is amplified enormously. Our minds are the information-processing mechanisms of an organism interacting with a particular environment via certain particular senses (natural endowments, hardware) and certain culturally evolved methods (cultural endowments, software). With different sorts of beings, these resources would differ profoundly—and so would the cognitive products that flow from their employment. Given intelligent beings with a physical and cognitive nature profoundly different from ours, one simply cannot assert with confidence what the natural science of such creatures would be like. That it would be different is clear, how it would be different is practically unfathomable.

It may seem tempting to reason: 'Since there is only one nature, only one science of nature is possible.' Yet, on closer scrutiny, this reasoning becomes highly problematic. Above all, it fails to reckon with the fact that while there indeed is only one world, nevertheless very different *thought-worlds* can be at issue in the elaboration of a 'science'.

Our alien scientific colleagues scan nature for regularities, using (at any rate, to begin with) the sensors provided them by their evolutionary heritage. They note, record, and transmit those regularities that they find to be useful or interesting, and then develop their inquiries by theoretical triangulation from this basis. Now, this is clearly going to make for a course of development that closely gears their science to their particular situation—their biological endowment ('their natural sensors'), their cultural heritage ('what is interesting'), and their environmental niche ('what is pragmatically useful'). Where these key parameters differ, we must expect that the course of scientific development will differ as well.

Admittedly, there is only one universe, and its laws and materials are, as best we can tell, the same everywhere. We share this common universe with all life-forms. However radically we differ in other respects (in particular, those relating to environment, to natural endowments, and to style or civilization), we have a common background of cosmic evolution and a common heritage of natural laws. And so, if intelligent aliens investigate nature at all, they will investigate the same nature we ourselves do. But the sameness of the object of contemplation does nothing to guarantee the sameness of ideas about it. It is all too familiar a fact that even where only human observers are at issue, very different constructions are often placed upon 'the same' occurrences. As is clearly shown by the rival interpretations of different psychological schools—to say nothing of the court testimony of rival 'experts'—there need be little uniformity in the conceptions held about one selfsame object from different 'perspectives of consideration'. Whatever the laws of, say, motion, or of chemistry are, they will be the same always, everywhere, and for anyone. But that is not of course to say that intelligent beings will always, everywhere, and unanimously have the same *conception* of them (or, indeed, any conception at all). The fact that all intelligent beings inhabit the same physical universe does not countervail the no less momentous fact that we inhabit very different ecological niches within it, engendering very different sorts of *modus operandi*, physical and cognitive alike. They do—nay, given their situational difference, *must*—think about the world differently from ourselves. And this difference is not just one of chance and fact but one of which is, in the circumstances, the rationally appropriate response.

It is surely naïve to think that because one single object is in question, its description must issue in one uniform result. This view ignores the crucial impact of the describer's intellectual orientation. Minds with different concerns and interests and with different experiential backgrounds can deal with the selfsame items in ways that yield wholly disjoint and disparate results because different features of the thing are being addressed. Epistemologists have often said things to the effect that people whose experience of the world is substantially different from our own are bound to conceive of it in very different terms. Sociologists, anthropologists, and linguists talk in much the same terms, and philosophers of science have recently also come to say the same sorts of things. Thomas Kuhn, for example, tells us that scientists who work within different scientific traditions—and thus operate with different descriptive and explanatory 'paradigms'—actually 'live in different worlds'.[7] The *things* that confront them may be the same, but their *significance* is altogether different.

[7] Thomas Kuhn, *The Structure of Scientific Revolutions* (Chicago, 1962).

The development of a 'science'—a definite codification of the laws of nature—always requires as input some inquirer-supplied element of determination. The result of such an interaction depends crucially on the contribution from both sides—from nature and from the intelligences that interact with it. A kind of 'chemistry' is at work in which nature provides only one input and the inquirers themselves provide another—one that can massively and dramatically affect the outcome in such a way that we cannot disentangle the respective contributions of nature and the inquirer. Things cannot of themselves dictate the significance that an active intelligence can attach to them. Human organisms are essentially similar, but there is not much substantive similarity between the medicine of the ancient Hindus and that of the ancient Greeks.

These considerations point to a clear lesson. Different civilizations composed of different sorts of creatures must be expected to create diverse 'sciences'. Though inhabiting the same physical universe with us, and subject to the same sorts of fundamental regularities, they must be expected to create as cognitive artefacts different depictions of nature, reflecting their different modes of emplacement within it.

Each inquiring civilization must be expected to produce its own, perhaps ever-changing, cognitive products—all more or less adequate in their own ways but with little if any actual overlap in conceptual content. There is no categorical assurance that intelligent creatures will *think* alike in a common world, any more than that they will *act* alike—that is, there is no reason why *cognitive* adaptation should be any more uniform than *behavioural* adaptation. Thought, after all, is simply a kind of action; and as the action of a creature reflects its biological heritage, so too does its mode of thought.

Natural science—broadly construed as inquiry into the ways of nature—is something that is in principle endlessly plastic. Its development will trace out a historical course closely geared to the specific capacities, interest, environment, and opportunities of the creatures that develop it. We are deeply mistaken if we think of it as a process that must follow a route generally parallel to ours and issue in a roughly comparable product. It would be grossly unimaginative to think that either the journey or the destination must be the same—or even substantially similar.

No one who has observed how very differently the declarations of a single text (the Bible, say, or the dialogues of Plato) have been interpreted and understood over the centuries—even by people of a common cultural heritage—can be hopeful that the study of a common object by different civilizations must lead to a uniform result. Yet, such textual analogies are oversimple and misleading, because the scientific study of nature is not a matter of decoding a pre-existing text. There just is not one fixed basic text—the changeless 'book of nature writ large'—which different civilizations can decipher in different degrees. Nature is to some extent a mirror: what looks out depends on who looks in.

Factors such as capacities, requirements, interests, and course of development affect the shape and substance of the science and technology of any particular cosmic civilization. Unless we narrow our intellectual horizons in a parochially anthropomorphic way, we must be prepared to recognize the great likelihood that the 'science' and 'technology' of a remote civilization would be something *very* different from science and technology as we know it. Our human sort of natural science may well be *sui generis*, adjusted to and co-ordinated with a being of our physical constitution, the characteristic product of a creature inserted into the orbit of the world's processes and history in our particular sort of way. In science, as in other areas of human endeavour, we are prisoners of sorts, confined within the thought-world that our biological, and social, and intellectual heritage affords us.

4.3 *Empiricism Entails Pluralism*

So much, then for experientially grounded pluralism on a cosmic scale. But, of course, the prime concern of these present deliberations is with something far more local, namely, the pluralism inherent in the variation of human experience here on earth. And it is clear that, even at this local level, the empirical basis of our factual knowledge is bound to engender a variety of alternative cognitive positions through the variation of experience. For the cognitive exploitation of different *bodies* of experiences—let alone different *sorts* of experience—is bound to lead rational inquirers to different results. Given the diversity of human experience, empiricism entails pluralism. The experiential diversity of differently situated rational inquirers must mean that they are destined to reach variant conclusions about the nature of things. In a human community of more than trivial size, dissensus rather than consensus is the normal condition.

In assessing the truth of substantively informative claims, inquirers do (and must) proceed on the basis of a 'perspective'—a 'cognitive stance' or 'point of view' regarding evidential/methodological matters from which the issues are judged. We cannot call upon the Recording Angel to inform us in matters of inquiry, but have to proceed with the instruments and materials at our disposal to make the best judgements that we can manage to achieve. We have to estimate—to devise informed conjectures—and we have different experiential bases for making such estimates. It is thus only normal, natural, and to be expected that people equipped with different courses of experience should judge differently with respect to issues that are not in themselves totally cut and dried.

The fact is that the realization of a consensus among inquirers requires extraordinarily unusual conditions—conditions of a special and particular sort which are not in general met in the difficult circumstances of an imperfect world. It is simply implausible and unrealistic to expect such a state of affairs to prevail with any frequency. To set the heart on consensus in our inquiries to ask for the unachievable.

The key point is that even where there is agreement about the aims of the cognitive enterprise ('determining the truth about how things work in the world'), and even where there is agreement about the appropriate means and methods for attaining this end (the scientific-inductive method), inquirers will nevertheless still arrive at discordant and conflicting results when the data afforded by the course of their experience are different—as differences in the times, societies, and circumstances render inevitable. And so, to re-emphasize: cognitive dissensus is rendered inevitable by experiential diversity among inquirers. Accordingly the pluralism that a sensible empiricism engenders in the light of such variable experiential conditions is rationally justified. The unavailability of consensus and the inescapability of cognitive pluralism are realities of the life of reason with which any satisfactory theory of knowledge has to come to terms.

5

Does Pluralism Lead to
Scepticism or Syncretism?

5.1 *The Question of Pluralism*

Even pluralism itself—the doctrine that any substantial
question admits of a variety of plausible but mutually
conflicting responses—lies open to a plurality of versions and
constructions. And epistemic pluralism in particular does so
in a way that raises the question of whether the truth is
something that admits not only of different *visions* but of
different *versions*, whether there are different and incompatible
truths or simply different and incompatible opinions regarding
the monolithic truth.

But this issue, however portentous in the abstract, has little
concrete bearing. It is in the deepest sense an *academic* one. For
we who exist as world-encompassed beings have no direct
access to The Truth—we can get there only through epistemic
mediation: our only access to the truth is via what we
conscientiously believe. We have no way of coming to grips
with the truth apart from what we think to be so on the basis
of such indications as we can get hold of. Thus while in the
abstract the distinction between visions and versions of the
truth may be all-important, nevertheless in the concrete, for
us here and now, it is a distinction without a difference. The
truth, like the Bible, may be one, but it is, again like the Bible,
a one that admits of many constructions and interpretations.
For all practical purposes—and for all *implementable* theoretical
purposes as well—a plurality of beliefs about the truth (a
plurality of visions) is a plurality of formulations of the true (a
plurality of versions). And this fact is something we must
somehow come to terms with.

TABLE 5.1. *Reactions to pluralism*

1. *Scepticism*	no alternative should be accepted: no single position at all justified; the alternatives simply cancel one another out
2. *Syncretism*	all the alternatives should be accepted: all those seemingly discordant positions are in fact justified; they must, somehow, be conjoined and juxtaposed
3. *Indifferentist Relativism*	only one alternative should be accepted, but this acceptance cannot be based on rationally cogent grounds but emerges from considerations that themselves lack any rational basis—as a matter of taste, of 'personal inclination', or social tradition, or some such
4. *Perspectival Rationalism or Contextualism*	only one alternative should be accepted, and this acceptance has a basis of rational cogency, albeit this basis may differ perspectivally from group to group, era to era, and school to school

Confronted with a variety of discordant positions, various reactions are in principle possible, as set out in Table 5.1.

This chapter and its successor will examine these various positions, arguing the case for avoiding scepticism, syncretism, and relativistic indifferentism. Accordingly, perspectival rationalism emerges in the end as the best and most cogent policy option, one that is rendered attractive by its substantial advantages over its rivals.

5.2 *The Defects of Scepticism*

Let us begin with scepticism. Already Xenophanes of Colophon, the pioneer of the Eleatic school of pre-Socratic philosophers who flourished around 540 BC, taught that people shaped their views of things divine no less than natural in a way that varies in line with the familiar fabric of their own experience: 'But if cattle and horses or lions had hands, or were able to draw with their hands and do the works that men can do, horses would draw the forms of the gods like horses, and cattle like cattle, and they would make their bodies such, as they each had themselves' (Frag. 169).[1] Experiential

---

[1] G. S. Kirk, J. F. Raven, and M. Schofield, *The Presocratic Philosophers*, 2nd edn. (Cambridge, 1983).

diversity leads different people—and, all the more, different groups and eras—to adopt different views. The idea that there are a variety of fundamental cognitive stances (perspectives, *Einstellungen*) towards the nature of things that engender different positions is thus virtually as old as philosophy itself.

The sceptics of classical antiquity inclined to see the various discordant philosophical doctrines as simply annihilating one another. Reacting to the idea that each culture looks at first principles from its own particular vantage point, Xenophanes already draw a sceptical conclusion: 'No man knows, or ever will know, the truth about the gods and about all the things I speak of; for even if he chanced to say the complete truth, yet oneself knows it not; but seeming is wrought over all' (Frag. 186). And this reduction of all vaunted knowledge to a 'mere seeming' is something that has enlisted the enthusiastic approbation of sceptics of all eras.

The last, culminating member of the series of sceptical tropes (*ho apo tēs diaphōnias*) propounded by Aenesidemos of Knosos, who flourished around 50 BC, construed the variation of people's views in philosophical matters to betoken a total incapacity to settle philosophical questions on a rational basis. As elaborated by Sextus Empiricus, who flourished around AD 150, this *trope* was seen as refuting dogmatism (i.e. philosophical conviction) in all its forms. It ran as follows:

There is a *Tenth Mode* [of sceptical argumentation], which is mainly concerned with Ethics, being based on rules of conduct, habits, laws, legendary beliefs, and dogmatic conceptions . . . Dogmatic conception is the acceptance of a fact which seems to be established by analogy or some form of demonstration, as, for example, that atoms are the elements of existing things, or homoeomeries, or *minima*, or something else. And each of these we oppose now to itself, and now to each of the others. For example, we oppose habit to habit in this way: some of the Ethiopians tattoo their children, but we [Greeks] do not . . . And among the Scythian Tauri it was a law that strangers should be sacrificed to Artemis, but with us it is forbidden to slay a human being at the altar . . . Since by means of this Mode also so much divergency is shown to exist in objects, we shall not be able to state what character belongs to the object in respect of its real essence, but only what belongs to it in respect of this particular rule of conduct, or law, or habit, and so on with each of the rest. So because of this Mode also we are compelled to suspend judgement regarding the real nature of external objects.[2]

In this way, the ancient sceptics inclined to see the variation of theological and philosophical thought among people as having destructively negative implications—as showing the futility and inappropriateness of the whole process of theorizing about first principles. Throughout the sceptical tradition, the variation of beliefs has been invoked to support a nihilism that takes a lack of consensus to betoken an absence of the objective factuality needed for rational belief, evaluation, and deliberation. The absence of guarantees in a situation that permits the prospect of different constructions, different interpretations or opinions, is taken to annihilate the matter in view as a meaningful issue.

But even as scepticism is an old doctrinal position, so is its rejection. And for good reason. For the sceptic too readily loses sight of the *raison d'être* of our cognitive endeavours. The object of rational inquiry is not just to avoid error but to answer our questions, to secure *information* about the world. And here, as elsewhere, 'Nothing ventured, nothing gained' is the operative principle. Granted, a systematic abstention from cognitive involvement is a sure-fire safeguard against one kind of error. But it affords this security at too steep a price. The shortcoming of that 'no risk' option is that it guarantees failure from the very outset. To put scepticism into a sensible perspective, it is useful to consider the issue of cognitive rationality in the light of risk-taking.

There are three very different sorts of approaches to risk, and three very different sorts of 'personality' corresponding to these approaches. The first type, 'risk-avoidance', is an approach that calls for risk aversion and evasion. Its adherents have little or no tolerance for risk and gambling. Their approach to risk is altogether negative. Their mottoes are 'Take no chances,' 'Play safe,' 'Always expect the worst'. The second type is a 'risk-calculating' approach that is somewhat more 'realistic'. It is a guarded, middle-of-the-road approach to risk, based on due care and calculation. It comes in two varieties:

---

[2] *Outlines of Pyrrhonism*, 1. 145–63.

1. The 'cautiously calculating' approach that sees risk-taking as subject to a negative, anti-presumption that can, however, be defeated by suitably large benefits. Its line is: 'Avoid risks unless it is relatively clear that a suitably large gain beckons at sufficiently auspicious odds.' It reflects the path of prudence and caution.

2. The 'daringly calculating' approach that sees risk-taking as subject to a positive, pro-presumption that can be defeated by suitably large negativities. Its line is: 'Take risks unless it is relatively clear than an unacceptably large loss threatens at sufficiently inauspicious odds.' It reflects the path of optimism and sanguine hopefulness.

Finally there is the 'risk-seeking' approach that calls for the courting of risks. Its adherents close their eyes to the dangers and take a rosy view of risk situations. The mind of the risk-seeker is intent on the delightful consequences of a favourable issue of events: the sweet savour of success is already in his nostrils. Risk-seekers are chance-takers and go-for-broke gamblers. They react to risk the way an old war-horse responds to the sound of musketry: with eager anticipation and positive relish for the fray. Their motto is: 'Things will work out.'

In conducting their practical and cognitive affairs the risk-avoiders are hypercautious; with no stomach for uncertainty, they insist on playing it absolutely safe. In any potentially risky situation, the mind of the risk-avoider is given to imagining the myriad things that could go wrong. The risk-calculators proceed with care: they take due safeguards, but still run risks when the situation looks sufficiently favourable. The risk-seekers, on the other hand, leap first and look later, apparently counting on a benign fate to ensure that all will be well; they dwell in the heady atmosphere of 'nothing can go wrong'.

It is clear that, in cognitive matters, fervent risk-avoidance leads straight away to scepticism. The sceptic's line is: 'Run no risks of error; take no chances; accept nothing that does not come with iron-clad guarantees.' (And the proviso here is largely academic, seeing that little if anything in this world comes with iron-clad guarantees.) If we ask more of our cognitive sources than they can possibly deliver, then scepticism becomes inevitable.

In the appraisal of cognitive risks, two fundamentally different sorts of misfortune have to be taken into account:

Misfortunes of the first kind: We reject something that, as it turns out, we should have accepted. We decline to 'take the chance' and avoid running the risk at issue, but things turn out favourably after all, and we 'lose out on the gamble'.

Misfortunes of the second kind: We accept something that, as it turns out, we should have rejected. We do 'take the chance' and run the risk at issue, but things go wrong, and we 'lose the gamble'.

If we are risk-seekers, we will incur few misfortunes of the first kind, but—things being what they are—relatively many of the second kind will befall us. Conversely, if we are risk-avoiders, we shall suffer few misfortunes of the second kind, but shall inevitably incur relatively many of the first. The overall situation is depicted in Figure 5.1.

In the cognitive case, in particular, the sceptic succeeds splendidly in averting misfortunes of the second kind. By accepting nothing, he accepts nothing false. But, of course, he loses out on the opportunity to obtain any sort of information. The sceptic thus errs on the side of safety, even as the syncretist errs on that of gullibility.

In claiming that his position wins out because it makes the fewest mistakes, the sceptic uses a distorted system of scoring. For, while he indeed makes the fewest errors of one kind, he makes the most of another. Once we look on this matter of making mistakes realistically, the sceptic's vaunted advantage vanishes. The sceptic is simply a risk avoider who is prepared 'to take no risks' and stubbornly insists on minimizing errors of the second kind alone.

But, after all, what we want in inquiry—the object of the whole enterprise—is information. What we seek is the very best achievable overall balance between answers to our questions and ignorance or misinformation.

We face a trade-off at this stage, however. Are we prepared to run a greater risk of error to secure the potential benefits of greater understanding? The judicious cognitivist is a risk

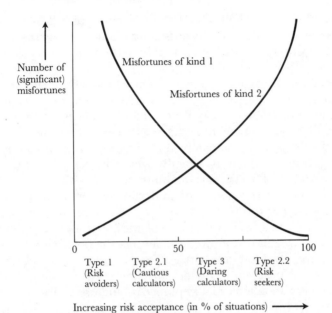

FIG. 5.1. *Risk acceptance and misfortunes*

calculator who recognizes the value of understanding and is prepared to gamble for its potential benefits. H. H. Price has put the salient point well:

'Safety first' is not a good motto, however tempting it may be to some philosophers. The end we seek to achieve is to acquire as many correct beliefs as possible on as many subjects as possible. No one of us is likely to achieve this end if he resolves to reject the evidence of testimony, and contents himself with what he can know, or have reason to believe, on the evidence of his own firsthand experience alone. It cannot be denied that if someone follows the policy of accepting the testimony of others unless or until he has specific reason for doubting it, the results will not be all that he might wish. Some of the beliefs which he will thereby acquire will be totally incorrect, and others partly incorrect. In this sense, the policy is certainly a risky one ... but it is reasonable to take this risk, and unreasonable not to take it. If we refuse to take it, we have no prospect of getting answers, not even the most tentative ones, for many of the questions which interest us.[3]

[3] H. H. Price, *Belief* (London, 1969), 128.

What Price says here about the testimony of others is even truer when applied to the testimony of our own senses.

It is simply self-defeating to follow the radical sceptic into letting discretion be the whole of epistemic valour by systematically avoiding accepting anything whatsoever in the domain of empirical fact. To be sure, when we set out to resolve a problem we may well discover in the end that, try as we will, success in reaching this goal is beyond our means. But we shall *certainly* get nowhere at all if we do not even set out on the journey—which is exactly what the sceptic's blanket proscription of acceptance amounts to.

In 'playing the game' of undertaking commitments and laying claims to credence, we may well lose; our problem-resolutions may well turn out to be mistaken. But, in a refusal to play this game at all we face not just the possibility but the certainty of losing the prize—we abandon any chance to realize our problem-resolving objectives. A sceptical policy of systematic avoidance of acceptance is fundamentally *irrational*, because it blocks from the very outset any prospect of realizing the inherent goals of the enterprise of factual inquiry.

In cognition, as in other sectors of life, there are no guarantees, no ways of averting risk altogether, no option that is totally safe and secure. The best and most we can do is to make optimal use of the resources at our disposal to 'manage' risks as best we can. To decline to do this by refusing to accept any sort of risk is to become immobilized. The sceptic thus pays a great price for the comfort of safety from errors of commission. If we want information—if we deem ignorance and indecision no less a negativity than error—then we must be prepared to 'take the gamble' of answering our questions in ways that risk some possibility of mistakes. The sensible thing is to adopt the 'middle-of-the-road' policy of risk calculation, acting as best we can to balance the positive risks of outright loss against the negative ones of lost opportunity. The path of reason calls for sensible calculation and prudent management: it standardly enjoins upon us the Aristotelian 'golden mean' between the extremes of risk-avoidance and risk-seeking. Rationality thus calls for taking the line: 'Neither avoid nor court risks, but manage them prudently in the endeavour to minimize misfortunes *overall*', and it insists on proceeding by way of carefully calculated risks that balance errors of commission and those of omission against one another. A middle-of-the-road evidentialism emerges as the most sensible approach.

The sceptic *seemingly* moves within the orbit of rationality, but only seemingly so. For, scepticism runs afoul of the only promising epistemological instrumentalities that we have. To be sure, there will have to be a justification for our epistemological procedures. And, if it were simply this rationalization that the sceptic asked for his demands would not be unreasonable—and could in principle be met. But, the defence itself would, of course, have to be conducted within the framework of the standard *modus operandi* of rational argumentation. There is and can be no rational justification outside the domain of rationality itself. The radical sceptic's demand for a justification of rationality *ex nihilo* is inappropriate because it defines its problem in such a way that any resolution is in principle infeasible. (Scepticism, as Hegel suggested, invited the response of a sceptic as regards its own merits.)

Homo sapiens has evolved within nature to fill the ecological niche of an intelligent being. The demand for understanding, for a cognitive accommodation to one's environment—for 'knowing one's way about'—is one of the most fundamental requirements of the human condition. Man is *homo quaerens*. We have questions and want (nay, *need*) answers. The need for information and thought-orientation in our environment is as pressing a human need as that for food itself. We are rational animals and must feed our minds even as we must feed our bodies, perforce settling for the best we can get at the time. The quest for cognitive orientation in a difficult world represents a deeply practical requisite for us. That basic demand for information and understanding presses in upon us and we must do (and are pragmatically justified in doing) what is needed for its satisfaction.

The tendency of scepticism is altogether nihilistic in response to our substantive question. It leaves us completely empty-handed. On its approach, every position is invalid, no one resolution of our cognitive or practical problems has any real merit over against another, so that irresolution is the only available course. On the basis of general principles, and without giving detailed inquiries a fighting chance, we are left in a position of total ignorance. Scepticism enjoins vacuity.

The only sort of critique of scepticism that it makes sense to ask for is a *rational* critique. And, viewed from this standpoint, the decisive flaw of scepticism is that it makes rationality itself impossible.

To be sure, merely theoretical argumentation cannot dislodge the sceptic from his stance of accepting no theses at all. Argumentation is unavailing because any probatively cogent *argument* must proceed from conceded premises and the sceptic can always simply refuse to make concessions. All that *argumentation* can do is to forestall scepticism by showing the incompatibility of sceptic with positions acceptable to sensible people in general. And this involves commitments which the sceptic has, of course, declined to undertake. Such argumentation will not dislodge someone from a sceptical position. But it should, at any rate, prevent somebody who has not already taken this position from doing so.

5.3 *Pluralism without Scepticism*

The idea that pluralism inexorably brings scepticism in its wake hinges on arguing that in those problematic situations where there are genuine alternatives, no rationally cogent basis is ever available for preferring one to the rest. But this reasoning on behalf of mutual cancellation of alternatives turns on the (clearly problematic) enthymematic premiss that where different individuals or groups opt for different alternatives, they do so with equal justification: that all of the options are equally good. And this premiss is very far from being available.

The fact that others may think differently from ourselves does little or nothing as such to preclude us from warranted confidence in the appropriateness and correctness of our own views. The idea that pluralism's recognition of the existence of other alternatives entails a sceptical suspension of opinion on the grounds of our being obliged to see the existence of other opinions as annihilating the tenability of our own is, to put it mildly, far-fetched.

Pluralism holds that it is rationally intelligible and accept-able that others can hold positions at variance with one's own. But it does *not* maintain that a given individual need endorse a plurality of positions—that the fact that others hold a certain position somehow constitutes a reason for doing so oneself.

Any viable proceeding in this range of discussion must distinguish between the standpoint of the individual and the standpoint of the group. Pluralism is a feature of the collective group: it turns on the fact that different experiences engender different views. But from the standpoint of the individual this cuts no ice. We have no alternative to proceeding as best we can on the basis of what is available to us. That others agree with us is no proof of correctness; that they disagree, no sign of error.

A pluralistic diversity of conflicting positions certainly is no basis for scepticism. To refuse to discriminate—be it by accepting everything or by accepting nothing—is to avert controversy only by refusing to enter the forum of discussion. It betokens fecklessness and vacuity. The questions that confront us in rational inquiry are simply too pressing and too important to admit of any such cavalier dismissals as the sceptics would have us make. In trying to be equally open (or closed) to all the alternatives, we get nowhere. To see alternative possibilities as simply cancelling one another out is simply to abandon the project of inquiry and decision. This is something we do not—and should not—want to do, because the issues matter too much, are simply too important to us. And this sort of reaction to the issue of rational inquiry holds also with respect to rational evaluation and action.

The question of intellectual seriousness is pivotal through-out. Do we care? Do we *really want* to obtain the rationally best resolutions of our problems that we can manage to secure? And are we sufficiently committed to this goal of question-resolution to be willing to take risks for the sake of its achievement, risks of potential error, of certain disagreement, and of possible obloquy and reproach? If we lose the sense of legitimacy and become too fainthearted to run such risks, we must pay the price of abandoning the entire project of rational choice.

Each and every era produces people who, tired, or

disillusioned, or simply wanting to be different, have advocated abandoning the perennial quest for understanding—for
making sense of the world's complex and chaotic-seeming
phenomena. But this is a tendency of thought that never
will—never can—prevail. The urge to make sense of things is
too deeply ingrained in our nature—as a human need rather
than merely a human want.[4]

5.4 *Syncretism and its Defects*

In reaction to a pluralism that acknowledges the existence of
diverse alternatives, we encounter also the prospect of
syncretism—that somewhat desperate policy of accepting all
the alternatives, of seeing all alike as equally appropriate. The
sceptic rejects all available options, the syncretist goes to the
opposite extreme and endorses the whole lot. With radically
open-minded pluralism, the syncretist, like P. K. Feyerabend,
inclines to think that anything goes. He is uncritically
accepting, and stands ready to endorse everything and to see
good on all sides. The evidentialist, by contrast, conducts his
cognitive business with care and caution, regarding various
sorts of claims as perfectly acceptable, provided that the
evidential circumstances are duly favourable. The sceptic will
accept nothing, the evidentialist only 'the chosen few', the
syncretist inclines favourably towards virtually everything.
What can be said of the status and standing of this response?

Facing a plurality of contending rival answers to our
questions, the sceptic embargoes *all* the available options and
enjoins us to reject the whole lot as meaningless or otherwise
inappropriate. The syncretist's option, more radical, though
equally egalitarian, is to proceed in the exactly opposite way
and view all the alternatives positively, embracing the whole
lot of them. The guiding idea of this approach is that of
conjoining the alternatives. Such a syncretism represents an
attempt to 'rise above the quarrel' of conflicting doctrines,
refusing to 'take sides' by taking all the sides at once. It is a

---

[4] This discussion draws upon the author's *Scepticism* (Oxford, 1980). For an
interesting consideration of relevant issues see also John Kekes, *A Justification of
Rationality* (Albany, NY, 1976).

Will Rogers kind of pluralism that never met a position it
didn't like. Confronted by discordant possibilities, it embraces
them all in a generous spirit of liberalism that sees them all as
essentially correct. Each alternative is held to carry its small
burden of truth to the general and all-embracing amalgam of
the Truth.

In recent years, relativistically inclined philosophers have
been drawn increasingly to the syncretist view of reality as a
complex manifold of diverse thought-structures all of which
are perfectly 'true' in their own way, though each gets at only
one aspect of a complex reality. Confronted with contradictory beliefs or doctrines, we need not—on syncretism's
telling—see ourselves as constrained to make a choice among
them; we can and should *conjoin* them. Properly speaking,
there should not be a *pluralism* of alternative positions at all,
but one single, all-inclusive conjunction of positions, a grand
superposition that embraces them all. Each individual doctrine
represents but one sector of the whole—only the totality of
doctrines captures the whole truth.[5] The incompatability of
claims does *not* mean that one or another of them must be
denied. We must be open to 'the recognition of the *equal or
nearly equal adequacy* of a number of world theories and to a
recommendation that we do not fall into the dogmatism of
neglecting anyone of them' and perist 'in holding these . . .
[rival] theories in suspended judgement as constituting the
sum of our knowledge of the subject'.[6]

Acting on this generous sentiment, syncretism sees all the
rival positions as being justified. Truth is somehow large and
complex enough to accommodate contradictions. With Hegel
(and Nicholas of Cusa before him) we should reject the
'principle of non-contradiction' which maintains that the
truth is self-consistent. On the contrary, every party to a
conflict of contradiction, duly supplemented by its several
contradictory alternatives, is thereby also an essential part of
the overall body of truth. Each self-consistent component is in

---

[5] The conjunctionist shares the sentiment with Tristram Shandy's father: ' 'Tis a
pity, said my father, that Truth can only be on one side, brother Toby—considering
what ingenuity these learned men have all shown in their solutions' (Laurence Sterne,
Tristram Shandy, bk. 3, ch. 41).

[6] Stephen C. Pepper, *World Hypotheses* (Berkeley, Calif., 1942), 342.

itself imperfect, limited by its very lack of contradictoriness from providing for the truths embodied in its contraries. Such a theory of multiple truth is an enlarged version of the medieval 'Averroist' theory of double truth, which held that reality embraces two incompatible world pictures, that of Aristotelian thought and that of Christian teaching. Syncretism propounds a conjoining of alternatives that lets everyone be right *on the whole*, a superdoctrine that lets all the contesting parties have their own ways throughout the entire range of doctrinal divergence. Such a position-*conjoining* approach is *not* a position-*combining* eclecticism of an internally diversified stance that each lower-level doctrine is right in some very partial, merely aspectival respect though wrong in others. Rather, it proposes to accept everything *as it stands*, without resorting to the 'interpretative' qualifications or emendations that reconcile discordant views via distinctions.

Syncretism's conjunctionist programme is guided by the model of the book and the library. The book should be consistent; it should tell its own internally coherent story. But, just as the library as a whole contains many diverse and discordant books, so reality is a complex of many different and discordant 'worlds'. Each has it own consistent and coherent rational structure. But reality is a complex and diversified whole that encompasses them all. Each particular doctrine presents its own thought-picture, and reality as a whole is ample enough to embrace them all without being confined to any of them, refusing to be captured in any one-sidedly self-consistent frame of thought. This sort of syncretism is the approach of the overly open-minded philosopher who, carried away by Hegel or Marx, simply 'refuses to take contradiction seriously'. Declining to be intimidated by mere inconsistency, he accepts mutually exclusive alternatives and revels in their very inconsistency, regarding it as a sign of the fecundity of the real. Presented with the choice between having his cake and eating it, he proposes to do both.

Syncretism too is an old position—and one closely allied to scepticism. The sceptic sees all alternative positions as equally unacceptable, the syncretist as equally acceptable. Protagoras is reported to have taught that everything can be disputed equally on both sides, pro and con—even whether everything is disputable on both sides ('Protagoras ait de omni re in utramque partem disputari posse ex aequo, et de hac ipsa, an omni res in ultramque partem disputabilis sit').[7] Here one cannot but wonder whether it is 'equal *force*' or 'equal *validity*' that is at issue—a question which Seneca's unqualified 'equally' (*ex aequo*) leaves frustratingly obscure. But be this as it may, the fact remains that those philosophers of classical antiquity who concerned themselves with the pluralistic variation of human opinion all construed the situation in an egalitarian sense. Either with the nihilistic sceptics, they wanted to reject all the alternatives, or with the syncretist sophists they wanted to accept them all, duly amalgamated in one indiscriminate mass.

Among the most ardent recent defenders of such a syncretism in the present century was the Spanish philosopher Ortega y Gasset (1883–1955).[8] As he viewed the matter, the historical course of thought and inquiry always brings forth a great variety of views and ideas on any given issue—each presenting an issue in a different and distinct perspective. Only the sum total of these perspectives adequately presents the full truth regarding the matter at issue, each partial perspective itself being incomplete, inadequate, distorted:

In this way, the characteristic peculiarity of every cognizing being, its individual make-up, far from preventing its grasp of the truth, is precisely the organ by which it sees that fragmentary part of the truth that corresponds to it. In this way, every individual, every generation, every epoch functioning as an instrument for attaining a unique item of knowledge. . . . [Only] through the partial visions of all can the complete and absolute truth be woven together.[9]

For Ortega, the 'God's eye view' of reality that achieves the ultimate of rational adequacy is not that of a perspective above and beyond the imperfect views of finite knowers, but rather is the entire collective sum-total aggregate of these partial views. This approach typifies the sort of philosophical syncretism that has become fashionable in the twentieth century.

---

[7] Seneca, *Epistles*, 88. 43.
[8] See especially *El Espectador* (Madrid, 1916).
[9] Ortega y Gasset, *Obras* (Madrid, 1932), 788.

One important point to be stressed is that a syncretist *conjunction* of positions is not a *synthesis*. Synthesis is the construction of a combining standpoint that mixes a piece of one position with some different piece of another—that grants one the right in *this* respect and another the right in *that* one. This sort of fusion, however, simply involves the adoption of yet another particular albeit pragmatic standpoint. The synthesist seeks somehow to co-ordinate dissonant positions in grand all-embracing synthesis. But of course every standpoint (perspective, doctrinal stance), however 'synthetic' it may be is just exactly that—just one more particular standpoint. And a combination-standpoint will also—in so far as it is possible at all—be just one more possible standpoint, just one more alternative in the overall spectrum. In so far as different standpoints admit of a synthesis (and strictly incompatible standpoints, though combinable in various ways, clearly cannot be amalgamated by way of conjunction) the result is no more than the adoption of just another standpoint. Synthesism is accordingly something quite different from syncretism—and something which does not, as such, take us outside the realm of particular and potentially divergent positions.

The syncretist does not avoid particular options but effectively adopts one. His position, like that of the sceptic, has a striking aura of self-inconsistency about it. This is illustrated by the very issue that underlies syncretism itself. How many alternative answers to a problematic question can possibly qualify as appropriate? Is it to be 0, 1, or $n > 1$? To respond *all of the above*—as a syncretist self-consistently must—does not really answer the question at all. Syncretism is in the end self-defeating, for it cannot avoid seeing the alternatives to itself (scepticism, absolutism, etc.) as equally valid. In being all-embracing it renders itself declaratively empty. *Affimare est negare.* Generous though it may sound, syncretism is accordingly not a very promising reaction to the reality of pluralism. For there just is no rationally sensible way in which to 'have it all ways at once'.

The grand idea of an intellectual symphony, where each player contributes to the overall harmony by playing his own score, is in deep difficulty simply because diverse doctrinal positions—discordant theses and theories—are, as they stand, logically inconsistent with each other. The result of juxtaposing them is bound to yield not music but cacophony.[10]

Syncretism's façade of openness and liberality hides from view the awesome cost of taking this sort of position. It purchases the advantage of being liberal and non-judgemental at an unacceptable price: in being over-generous, it is self-defeating. Seemingly it allows everything, but actually, when all is said and done, it puts us in exactly the same position as scepticism—we are left with . . . nothing!

5.5　Pluralism without Syncretism

Life being what it is, the community as a whole is bound to adopt inconsistent views. The *conjunction* of these mutually incompatible positions is not a coherent position—it is just a mess. Given a question of some sort ('Is *p* true?' for example), it just is not very helpful to be told 'It is and it isn't.' The conjunction of alternative possibilities simply cannot provide meaningful information. We institute inquiry to get answers to our questions. To have instead a survey of possible answers together with the assurance that all of them are 'in their own way, perfectly correct' is futile, meaningless, pointless. We don't get a tenable and informative position until we clean the mess up, until we remove the inconsistency and fashion some coherent doctrine out of it. Whatever the communal product of theorists at large may be, it is not a theory, any more than the communal product of diplomatists at large constitutes a diplomacy.

To refuse to discriminate—be it by accepting everything or by accepting nothing—is to avert controversy only by refusing to enter the forum of discussion. If we accept nothing then that is just what we get—nothing. And if we accept everything, we have to realize that this is not a way of taking a

---

[10] A useful and historically well-informed critique of *philosophical* syncretism is given in the section, 'Allegemeiner Nachweis der Unmöglichkeit einer all-umfassenden Einheits-philosophie', in Franz Kröner, *Die Anarchie der philosophischen Systeme* (Leipzig, 1929; repr. Graz, 1970), 131–52. See also the author's *The Strife of Systems* (Pittsburgh, 1985).

(particularly sophisticated) position but a way of avoiding the subject. In trying to be equally open (or closed) to all the alternatives, our deliberations are stymied. To transmute inquiry into the study of plausible-seeming alternatives is indeed to avoid doctrinal commitment, but it is also an abandonment of the arduous but productive path of a rational choice which alone prevents our coming away empty-handed from the deliberations at issue.

Given syncretism's shortcomings, it is fortunate that pluralism as such certainly does not engender this position. The fact that a plurality of different alternatives is available does not mean that we have to see them all as equally correct and adoptable and requiring to be conjoined and contrived. There is no earthly reason why a pluralism which, realistically, sees that the cognitive, practical, and evaluative issues that confront us all admit of several possible solutions, should deem itself impotent to effect a preferential choice among them. Only from a position of totally spineless choice-avoidance is the move from pluralism to an all-accepting syncretism possible.

To obtain informative guidance from question-resolving inquiry, it is not enough to this end to *contemplate* positions—be it as historical actualities or as theoretical possibilities. We must actually *commit* ourselves to one. We can only resolve our cognitive or practical problems if we conduct our inquiries in the doctrinalist manner—only if we are willing to 'stick our necks out' and take a position that endorses some answers and rejects others. And we can only do this in a reasonable way if we are willing to deploy the resources of reason in this process.

5.6 *Is Pluralism Self-Refuting?*

As pluralism sees it, a variety of distinct, mutually incompatible resolutions on any controvertible issue is in principle 'available'. But of course such a pluralism is itself but one among various alternatives (nihilism and monism among them). So far, then, pluralism is rather self-confirming than otherwise.

But if one maintains that pluralism is correct—or at any

rate more plausible or appropriate than its rivals—is not *thus* a position itself at odds with the spirit of pluralism? By no means.

There is, after all, no good reason why one's approach to pluralism should not be selectively rationalistic. Quite to the contrary. Consider again the situation of Table 5.1—which outlines the alternatives of scepticism, syncretism, indifferentist relativism, and contextualistic rationalism. The very question under discussion—how to respond to pluralism?—exemplifies the sort of pluralistic stance at issue with a choice among alternatives. But the sceptic, in rejecting all the alternatives, dishes his own position along with the rest. The syncretist abnegates any basis for maintaining his own position *vis-à-vis* its rivals. And the indifferentist insists that there is no good reason for adopting his solution rather than any other. Only preferential rationalism is able to address the issue satisfactorily within the framework of its own principles.

As has been argued throughout, nothing whatsoever inheres in pluralism as such that requires it to be *indifferentist* in seeing all those various available alternatives as being equally meritorious from the rational point of view. Such an indifferentism constitutes a position of *relativism* that plunges beyond pluralism to an extent that compromises its self-consistency. By contrast, a pluralism that is co-ordinated with a rational preference based on context-relevant considerations can be perfectly self-consistent—a consideration which surely constitutes a cogent reason for preferring this line of approach.

However, in this context of indifferentist relativism a further series of complex issues opens up before us that amply deserve a chapter unto themselves.

6

Pluralism without Indifferentism

6.1 *Against Indifferentist Relativism*

There are many different versions of monism/pluralism, depending on which approach to the question is taken, as in Table 6.1. Our prime concern thus far has been with matters of substantive and evaluative consensus or dissensus. And the sort of pluralism that is viable here is, clearly, one that is *not* indifferentistic—one that allows some positions (and itself in particular) to have a preferentially privileged status. Yet how can such a position be validated?

Consider the following two basic questions:

Q1: In general, how many of the alternatives with respect to a controverted matter are *plausible* in the sense of deserving sympathetic consideration and deliberation?

Q2: Within the range of such viable alternatives, how many are *acceptable* in the sense of deserving endorsement and adoption?

The range of answers to these questions is surveyed in Table 6.2.

Faced with a situation of dissensus involving a pluralistic proliferation of alternative positions, the sceptic rejects them all as untenable, and the syncretist embraces the entire lot. But yet another very different sort of reaction is possible—the *irrationalistic* preferentialist is someone who says: 'To be sure, it will not do to reject or accept all alternatives alike: we must indeed choose among the various positions. But which of them we opt for is *rationally* indifferent—it is merely a matter of taste, or habit, or inclination, or the influence of our teachers,

TABLE 6.1.

Conceptual	with a view to different concept-schemes, different ways for people to conceptualize their experience
Substantive	with a view to different belief systems, different ways for people to form their beliefs about truth and reality
Logical	with a view to different processes of reasoning and inference*
Methodological	with a view to different inquiry procedures, different criteria and standards of acceptability
Ontological	with a view to different realities, different bodies of *actual truths* (in contrast to different bodies of putative truths as per substantive pluralism)
Evaluative or axiological	with a view to different ways and means of evaluation
Practical	with a view to different types of interest and benefit

* Even in matters of conceptualization and inference—i.e. in logic and information processing (and mathematics as well)—these are real alternatives. On the relevant issues see the author's *Many-Valued Logic* (New York, 1969) and also N. Rescher and Robert Brandom, *The Logic of Inconsistency* (Oxford, 1980). Reference to the considerable literature of non-standard logic is given in these works.

TABLE 6.2. *A taxonomy of positions*

Range of answers		Resultant doctrinal position
Question 1	Question 2	
0	0	Nihilism
1	1	Monism (absolutism)
2 or more		Pluralism
	0	Scepticism
	1	Preferentialism
		Doctrinalism (rationalistic)
		Relativism (irrationalistic)
	2 or more	Syncretism

or the like.' This approach sees each of different alternative positions as being, from the *rational* point of view, equally valid—just as acceptable and appropriate as any other. Choice there indeed is, but only a rationally indifferent choice relative to a rationally immaterial basis of some sort, residing in a factor which, like individual psychology, group instruction, social custom, ideology, or the like, is extra-rational in nature. In modern times this reason-indifferentism—that is, *relativism*—has afforded the most common response to doctrinal pluralism. As it views the matter, there is indeed choice, but only one that is reason-indifferent in that it proceeds on a basis disjoint from the matter of good reasons. From the perspective of rationality, however, such a position is profoundly indifferentist. And only if we see rationality itself as a bogeyman—if we adopt a Feyerabendian 'anything goes' line—could such indifferentism look plausible. (And why in heaven's name should we do so?—a question to which no cogent answer can be forthcoming from a position that insists on abandoning cogency and rejecting all prospect of reason-giving.)

Again, when the theme of pluralism comes on the scene—when different people or groups adopt distinct and incompatible positions—two sorts of question arise: (1) How are we to evaluate these positions on our own account? Are we to dismiss those that differ from the one we ourselves favour, or are we to see them all as deserving of consideration and some positive response presumably stopping short of actual acceptance? (2) How are we to evaluate the posture of those who adopt those variant-positions? Are we to acknowledge that they are (or may be) proceeding in a way that is appropriate and legitimate given their situation and circumstances? These two issues are clearly different and distinct. And even if we are fully committed to the correctness of our position in some sphere (the medicine of our own day, for example) we may nevertheless acknowledge that other people (the Greeks of Galen's day, for instance) are fully entitled and rationally justified *given their situation*, in holding the views that they do.

The fact is, however, that recent discussions of these issues have been beclouded by a lack of clarity as to the nature of the issues and, in particular, by a failure to distinguish between pluralism (as a general, schematic position) and relativism (as a particular, irrationalistic version thereof). The salient points are: (1) That pluralism is compatible with preferentialism: seeing a range of alternative positions as deserving of our respect, consideration, and the like, is perfectly consistent with seeing only one of them as having a valid claim to our acceptance. (2) That a rationalistic preferentialism (i.e. doctrinalism) which insists on the correctness of one particular alternative is perfectly compatible with a pluralism that acknowledges that others, situated differently from ourselves in the experiential scheme of things, may be fully rationally warranted and entitled to hold the variant position they in fact adopt.

In every area of rational inquiry judgement rests on some basis of potentially variable data and methods, a basis that differs from one context to another because of the variation of experience of the inquiries involved. For the rationally appropriate exploitation of their differential experiences is bound to lead rational people into different directions. This contextual empiricism makes for an inner pluralism of rational process in not only authorizing, but even mandating, that differently situated inquirers should proceed differently. This variability in the operation of rational constraints is not a violation but a mandate of rationality. It is emphatically *not* a relativism that envisages a rationally unconstrained choice among indifferent alternatives. There is a vast—and for our present purposes—decisive difference between a rationalistic contextualism, on the one hand, and an indifferentistic relativism, on the other. The crucial point is that the absence of consensus simply is not—in the very logic of the situation— a decisive impediment to rational validity and impersonal cogency.

Of course, there are cognitive positions and approaches different from ours—different sorts of standards altogether. But what does that mean *for us*? What are *we* to do about it? Several stances towards the alternatives are in theory open to us:

1. accept none: reject all, ours included;
2. accept one: retain ours;
3. accept several: conjoin others with ours;
4. 'rise above the conflict': say 'a plague on all your houses' to the available alternatives and look elsewhere—to the 'ideal observer', to the 'wise man' of the Stoics, to the 'ideally rational agent' of the economists, or some such (in *these* circumstances unavailable) idealization.

The first option is mere petulance—a matter of stalking off in 'fox-and-grapes' fashion because we cannot have it all our own preferred way. The third option is rationally infeasible: different bases do not combine, they make mutually incompatible demands, and in *conjoining* them we will not get something more comprehensive and complete—we will get a mess. The fourth option is utopian and unrealistic: we have no way to get there from here. Only the second option makes sense: to have the courage of our convictions and stand by our own guns.

The salient point is that one cannot consistently both stake a claim to the rational validity of one's views and at the same time reject all commerce with rational standards and criteria. In this regard, our commitment to our own cognitive position is (or should be) unalloyed. We can and should see our own (rationally adopted) standards as superior to the available alternatives—and are, presumably, rationally entitled to do so by seeing them as *deserving* of preference on the basis of the cognitive considerations we ourselves can rationally endorse.

It deserves to be stressed that the pluralist who acknowledges the prospect of a variety of distinct positions with respect to cognitive, practical, or evaluative issues—each perfectly appropriate relative to one or another perspective basis—has no need whatsoever to consider all those different alternatives as equally meritorious from the standpoint of rational appraisal. Pluralists can see themselves as (like almost everyone) equipped with a judgemental basis whose impetus enables, nay *requires* them to adjudge some alternatives as superior to others *for good and sufficient reasons*. After all, even if we are pluralists and accept a wide variety of positions as being (abstractly speaking) available to people, we still retain the perfectly plausible prospect of evaluating our own particular (carefully deliberated) position as rationally superior. Indeed, if we *have* a position at all, this lies precisely in the fact that we see it as rationally cogent. The only ultimately tenable form of pluralism is one that is preferentialistically bound to a mechanism of rational appraisal on the basis of good reasons—a *rationalistic* preferentialism that looks to a privileged alternative underwritten by considerations of reason (rather than, say, by merely psychological or social considerations). What we want, after all, is a position we ourselves can see as rationally appropriate.

A preferentialistic pluralism of evaluative standards emphatically rejects the idea that the adoption of one doctrinal position rather than another is no more than 'a mere matter of taste', a fortuitous and ultimately irrationalizable preference, akin to that for coffee over tea. To take this line would be to ride roughshod over the fundamental distinction between mere *tastes and preferences* on the one hand and authentic *values* on the other. For the reasoned choice of a position hinges on the adopting of certain standards that are rooted in cognitive values. And to think of values in terms of taste-dependent preferences is to have a peculiar and distorted perception of values. Values are not irrationalizable. A perfectly good rational defence of one's cognitive value-system can be built up, but such a defence will itself have to be value-geared—and thus not without an element of probative circularity. People can in principle and often do in practice hold their values (cognitive ones included) for perfectly good reasons—albeit always reasons that themselves are ultimately evaluative in nature, and thus potentially variable.

Relativism is predicated on an indifferentism which maintains that whenever various bases of judgement, different evidential/evaluative standpoints or perspectives exist, then all these are (at least roughly) equally acceptable, so that there is no rationally cogent basis for choosing one rather than another. This position has it that such a choice, if made at all, must be based on extra-rational considerations—taste, custom, fashion, or the like. But good sense simply blocks the path to this destination in its demand that we attune our judgements to the structure of our own experiences, because anything else would be *irrational*. In the realm of thought as in that of physical nature we have no alternative but to work with the materials that the world's realities put at our disposal.

The decisive defect of epistemic relativism lies in its flat-out refusal to commit itself to the existence of impersonally cogent standards for our claims to knowledge. For someone who makes such a contention in a serious way clearly intends this claim to be viewed with favour—impersonally and by anyone.

They do not intend an *avowal* ('I happen to think that . . .'), nor yet a collective *report* ('We who belong to the group *G* think that . . .').

To put forward a position of one's own in a serious way as rationally tenable is to purport this position to be validatable by adequate and cogent reasons. Right or wrong, this is the claim that one implicitly stakes. And the relativist concession, 'My basis for making this claim is ultimately no better than other, conflicting bases that may well underwrite other, conflicting conclusions' is simply incompatible with it. Relativism accordingly puts the prospect of advancing a seriously intended, rationally cogent claim beyond one's reach. It makes it impossible to put forward *any* such claim or contention—that of relativism itself included. Seen as a serious doctrinal position, relativism is simply self-undermining. It lies in its very nature that it is self-frustrating in that to whatever extent it is correct it cannot be seriously maintained to be so. Any concern for the *merits* of relativism introduces the relativistic difficulties. One asks, 'What can one make of the acceptability claims of this position?' And what is at issue here are clearly claims to *cogency*—to *validity*. But note the irony here. On relativism's own telling, no such normative claims can possibly be made good. For reasons of simple self-consistency, indifferentist relativism can advance no claims on its own behalf. But a position that makes no claim is for that very reason . . . pointless.

To be rational consists (*inter alia*) in seeing one's own framework as privileged in that it was just exactly for this reason—its superior substantiation—that one chose it in the first place, namely, because one has good reason to see it as rationally appropriate. Only by our taking this sort of stance towards our own cognitive framework can the position that we ourselves hold avoid cognitive dissonance and vacuity.

There is a very limited utility to the observation that a certain thesis *p* holds relative to a certain framework of standards and criteria of acceptability *F*. For when our interest is in *p* itself, it is little to the purpose to be informed that *F* endorses *p*. The fact that *p* holds relative to *F* tells us nothing about *p* as such. Only to the extent that we are prepared to accept the criteriology of *F* as cogent and appropriate can we make any steps from F's endorsement of p towards p itself. The situation is much akin to that of testimonial endorsement from a human source. Only in so far as we deem this source to be cognitively credit-worthy—can we move inferentially from its endorsement to the claim itself.

Accordingly, framework-relative assertion is one thing and assertion as such another. We certainly do not in general have the equivalence

$p \longleftrightarrow p$ holds in F

But of course this equivalence does hold in the special case where F is F^*, the probative framework that we ourselves adopt. We have no choice but to see *our* truth as the *truth*. (It is, after all, just exactly in our taking this position that a contention's qualifying as 'our truth' consists.) To be sure at the level of generality we do not subscribe to

(Aq) $(q \longleftrightarrow q$ holds in $F^*)$

But at the level of concreteness—for any *particular* p, we have no choice but to endorse

$p \longleftrightarrow p$ holds in F^*

This must be seen as a conceptually authorized thesis, not, to be sure, of *logic* but of *epistemology*.

Yet, does perspectival pluralism not put everyone's position on exactly the same plane? Well, yes and no. The position does indeed see alternative philosophical positions as enjoying a parity of status from an *external* point of view; all responsibly developed positions are valid from a suitably favourable cognitive-value orientation and indefensible if we proceed from no orientation at all. But this externalized parity cannot be transmuted into an argument against such commitments—cannot be made over into a reason for not accepting them at all. For individuals do, in general, have a cognitive orientation and are able to resolve issues by its means. (The fact that words are meaningless until people endow them with meaning does not entail that they continue to be meaningless once they have done so.)

Accordingly, perspectival pluralism as such does not entail a relativistic indifferentism. Even if we are pluralists and

accept a wide variety of perspectives as being (abstractly
speaking) 'available', we still have no serious alternative to
seeing our own stance as superior—at any rate, if we have
such a stance at all, as we must do if we are actually
philosophizing. Faced with a variety of philosophical perspectives, the only sensible and appropriate course is to proceed on
the basis of the one that in fact enjoys our allegiance for the
sorts of reasons that we can and do accept as cogent. A
sensible pluralistic doctrination is not self refuting but rather
in principle self-sustaining.

It is difficult, after all, to bring oneself to see relativistic
arationalism in a favourable light. Its decisive defect is that it
commits an inherently inappropriate assimilation of all
standards to mere matters of *taste*. The issues controverted
between philosophical positions are transparently important;
indeed they are the most *momentous* issues that confront us in
the intellectual endeavour. A view that regards resolving these
massive issues as lying outside the sphere of reason, as
the product of rationally immaterial factors, is patently
problematic.

6.2 *A Foothold of One's Own*

Over the last century, indifferentist relativism has gathered
strength from various modern intellectual ventures. As the
sciences of man developed in the nineteenth century—especially in historical and sociological studies—the idea increasingly gained acceptance that every culture and every era has
its own characteristic fabric of thought and belief, each
appropriate to and cogent for its own particular context but
devoid of any larger validation. In particular, historicist
thinkers from Dilthey onwards have lent the aid and comfort
of their authority to a historico-cultural relativism of some
sort. Sociologists and anthropologists came from every corner
of the globe bearing tales of vastly different forms of social
organization and interaction that served perfectly well in the
societies in which they were entrenched. And the aftermath of
Darwinian biology reinforced this tendency of thought in
giving currency to the idea that our human view of reality is

formatively dependent upon our characteristically human cognitive endowments—as opposed to those of other possible sorts of intelligent creature. Not only do the data that we can acquire about the world come to us by courtesy of the biological endowment of our senses, but the inferences we can draw from those data will analogously be dependent on the biological endowment of our minds. Various turn-of-the-century philosophers of otherwise very diverse doctrinal orientations—ranging from Nietzsche and Vaihinger to Bergson and Samuel Alexander—all drew heavily on Darwinian inspirations to support a syncretist perspectivism of one sort or another.

The rise of anthropological studies brought further grist to relativism's mill. In the course of time, students of non-European and especially of 'primitive' cultures increasingly came to view each society as an embodiment of certain characteristic forms and values of its own. In seeking freedom from culture-bound prejudices, the anthropologist seems to have felt himself under an *ex officio* duty to view each culture as having a distinctive intellectual perspective—all of them to be valued equally because capable of being appraised only in the context of their own setting and context. And as psychology emerged as a new discipline in the late nineteenth century, it too lent aid and comfort to relativistic lines of thought—though now on a personalistic rather than culture-geared basis. Psychologists inclined to the line that there are different personality-types—each with its own characteristic set of needs, dispositions, and interests, and all of them of equal legitimacy and value. On this basis, psychologically inspired thinkers like William James and F. S. C. Schiller were also drawn to the development of a philosophical relativism.

Such examples show that many modern fields of study have brought grist to the mill of relativism. But its popularity notwithstanding, for those who have a serious stake in the enterprise at hand—be it cognitive, practical, or evaluative—such indifferentist relativism is a highly unattractive position. And pluralism certainly need not lead in its direction.

Perhaps from the point of view of the universe all experiential perspectives are of equivalent merit; and perhaps they are equal before God. But we ourselves cannot assume the prerogative of these mighty potencies. We humans can no more view cognitive issues with our minds without having a perspectival stance than we can view material objects with our bodily eyes without having a perspectival stance. But, of course, we ourselves do in fact occupy a particular position, with particular kinds of experience that equips us with particular issues and concerns and particular practical and intellectual tools for answering them. For us, accordingly, only one perspective stance can qualify as valid—the one we actually have. If we self-proclaimedly rational beings did not see it as being—uniquely—rationally valid, it would, *ipso facto*, not actually be *our* point of view, contrary to hypothesis.

In approving positions we have, of course, no alternative to doing so from the perspective of our cognitive posture—our own cognitive position and point of view. (It wouldn't *be* our point of view if we didn't use it as such.) And given its natural emergence from our own point of view, our doctrinal position is, of course, going to emerge as optimal on its own telling. (That *your* position is going to emerge as optimal on *your* orientation's telling is, of course, going to come to *me* neither as news nor yet as something intimidating.) It makes a crucial difference to everybody which position he or she adopts, though not in exactly the same way. We cannot maintain a posture of indifference. Each thinker, each school, is bound to take a strongly negative stand towards its competitors: belittling their concerns, deploring their standards, down-grading their values, disliking their presuppositions, scorning their contentions, and so on.

The heart and core of the anti-relativist position is the thesis that positions can be supported by standards of impersonal cogency—that they can be rationally justified in line with good reasons. Such a justificatory rationale of cogent standards and reasons must, as such, be 'universal'. But it is crucially important in this context to distinguish between universality of range ('universally valid for anyone') on the one hand and universality of endorsement ('universally accepted by every-one') on the other. For the very mistaken idea is abroad that a standard of impersonal cogency (a universally valid standard) must itself be impersonally and unrestrictedly *acknowledged* (a universally accepted standard)—that it must be the object of an effectively universal consensus. But these, of course, are very different things—in particular because people can be mis- or under-informed. The argument to relativism ('no universally cogent standards') from dissensus ('no universally accepted standards') simply shatters on the realities of the human epistemic condition. People being what they are (fallible, feckless, skittish, cantankerous, etc.), little—if anything—of substantiated significance is ever endorsed by everybody.

To re-emphasize: a pluralism of potential basis-diversity in rational inquiry is altogether compatible with an absolutistic commitment to our own basis. Admittedly, the rationally appropriate exploitation of their differential experiences is bound to lead rational inquirers in different directions. But one can certainly combine a relativistic pluralism of possible alternatives with a monistic position regarding ideal rationality and a firm and reasoned commitment to the standards intrinsic to one's own position. We ourselves are bound to see our own (rationally adopted) standards as superior to the available alternatives—and are, presumably, rationally entitled to do so in the light of the cognitive values we ourselves endorse. Rational is as rational does—it hinges on the norms, standards, and criteria that we ourselves can endorse as rationally appropriate on the basis of what best qualifies— from where we stand—as a well-considered position as to what is appropriate for anybody.

The step from a mere *pluralism* to an actual *relativism* can be taken only via an indifferentism that insists that there is really 'nothing to choose' between that plurality of distinct positions. But, of course, a choice can in theory be made via mere inclination, conformity to fashion, or any of a score of such reason-indifferent approaches. The core of an authentic relativism lies in its insisting that there is no *rationally cogent* way of choosing. Taking this stance, of course, does require a commitment to the idea that one can recognize a rationally cogent position when one sees one—that is, it demands an acknowledgement of rationality as such. But once this is conceded, then what price relativism? The position is a deeply problematic one that totters on the brink of incoherence.

But if there is no one single approach whose cogency is forced upon all alike through a 'position of reason alone'—no universally cogent probative perspective that must be acknowledged by all rational inquirers and no standard of rationality that transcends the experiential endowment of feeble humans—then where can we turn for our criteria of assessment in these matters? In the absence of the availability of such transcendental standards, it is clear that I can only appeal to *my* rationality. To assess rationality I must assess it as I see it, from where I stand. If I want to know if some way of proceeding is rational, I of course want to know if it is so in my sense of the term and by those standards and criteria that I myself endorse. The only standards it makes sense for me to use are those that I accept. And so for me there can in the end, be only my philosophy—any appeal to modes of reasoning or procedures for deciding issues, and the like that are not mine would be beside the point. If I do not *accept* them then my *use* of them would be pointless, intellectually dishonest, and philosophically self-defeating. What counts for me—and can alone do so—is my perspective on the rational explanation of experience.

Yet what *right* have you to persist in holding to your own perspective, maintaining your allegiance to your own standards and criteria in the face of the fact that others proceed differently? This question of right (entitlement, authorization) is not all that difficult to resolve, seeing that *right* here means 'rational justification'. For I will have such right just exactly in so far as I proceed rationally. And just as long as I proceed configuring my cognitive standards and criteria in a rationally conscientious way I shall, *ipso facto*, be rationally justified in holding and using them. After all, the rational configuration of one's standards and criteria exactly consists in this systematically congruent attunement to the realities of one's experience. That my standards should agree with those of others who are differently situated is not a requisite of reason but an absurdity. But nothing in this consideration goes to undermine the rational appropriateness of one's subscription to those standards.

But how, short of megalomania, can one take the stance that one's own view of what is rational is right—that it is something that is binding on everyone? How can I maintain this agreement between my position and that of 'all sensible people'? Not, surely, because I seek to impose *my* standard on *them*, but because I do—or should!—endeavour to take account of their standards in the course of shaping my own. Co-ordination is achieved not because I insist on their conforming to me, but because I have made every *reasonable* effort to make mine only that which (as best I can tell) ought to be everyone's. To this extent, the issue is not one of domineering but of submissive conformity. In the end, I can thus insist that they should use the same standard that I do because it is on this very basis of a commitment to commonality that I have made that standard my own in the first place. The conformity to rational standards is—or ought to be—produced not by megalomania but by humility.

The idea that 'we are entitled to our position' is ultimately inescapable if our position is one that is espoused rationally. But what if we have no position? Note in the first place that that is not a matter for the individual to decide about. What the standards of cognition or morality (etc.) are for the wider community to which we ourselves happen to belong is not something we can *decide* but something we find when we duly investigate. And then comparative cogency *vis-à-vis* alternatives is something we can also rationally investigate on the basis of teleological considerations. The crucial issue is not what we deem congenial but what we find effective: it is a matter not of *decision* but of *rational determination* by the one and only standard of rationality available to us—our own.

Cognitive relativism thus has its limits. The implications of our own conception of rationality are absolutely decisive for our deliberations. When the discussion at issue is one that we are conducting, then we ourselves must be the arbiters of relevancy and cogency. And so, we cannot at once maintain our own rational commitments as such, while yet ceasing to regard them as results at which all rational inquirers who proceed appropriately ought also to arrive if the circumstances were the same. In this sort of way, the inherent claims of rationality are universal, and if you will, absolute.

An orientational pluralism certainly does *not* propose to abandon the pursuit of truth. It simply enjoins us to recognize that, short of adopting standards of probative assessment, there is no way of conducting rational inquiry in this domain, and to acknowledge that such a posture is seldom if ever a community-wide universal. But, of course, *since we ourselves do have such a posture*, one that we presumably see as uniquely right and proper precisely because we have made it ours, we need not and should not be intimidated by the fact that others—poor benighted souls—might work matters out differently. An orientational pluralism does not entail in-differentism. In inquiry—as in morals or politics—the fact that one must inevitably defend one's position on the basis of one's values certainly does not impede our taking the stance that our position is right. (It is, after all, just such a commitment that makes a position into *our* position—if we are rational.)

An orientational pluralism of diverse normative perspectives grounded in different bodies of experience takes the following line:

> The choice between alternative positions is of interest and importance. We can and should make every effort to assure that, from our own standpoint, we have made the very best resolution that is available to us. And, from the rational point of view an attunement to 'available' experience taken overall indeed is the best that we can do in this regard. The fact that other resolutions are possible—resolutions that might well be adopted by others who appraise the issue differently—accordingly should not faze us for a moment. For we simply have to go on from where we are. Once we have done the best that can be done to provide for the rational accommodation of our experience, we may rest content. The fact that others with different bodies of experience might resolve the matter differently is simply *irrelevant* to our own resolution of the issues.

Once a cognitive-value orientation is in hand, only one member of the range of alternatives is (in general) optimally appropriate. (An orientational *monism* is the obverse side of orientational *pluralism*.) This sort of experiential pluralism certainly does not see the choice among alternatives as rationally indifferent. For on its approach, *experience* is seen as invariably position-determinative.

It is all very well to say 'To each their own—live and let live.' But in practical matters one agent's solutions create problems for others (e.g. by sending misinformation their way or, even worse, acid rain). The limits of *laissez-faire* are reached where impacts upon people's interests or well-being are at issue. And at this point we have no wish to follow any view but our own—and have no sensible alternative to doing so in the most conscientious way possible. To assess injury to people we must use our own standards, and, to avert it, our own convictions.

But what of pragmatism as a force for conformity and consensus? Do considerations of purpose efficacy and practical utility not render the choice among alternatives something that is objectively fixed and non-relative? Not necessarily! For while efficacy by *given* standards with respect to *given* purposes is indeed something objective and non-relative, the fact remains that purposes and standards themselves are unavoidably variable.

Such a situation prevails, however, only from the global perspective of 'the human situation' at large. We ourselves occupy a particular context. For our purposes the standards for their achievement are fixed by our unasked-for positions in the experiential scheme of things. And we have no choice but to go in from where we are.

One acute epistemic pragmatist suggests that: 'Just as there are many good ways to prepare food, or raise children, or organize a society, so too there may be many good ways to go about the business of cognition.'[1] This contention immediately raises the question. 'Many diverse ways that are "equally good" *for whom*?' That different people differently situated in varied circumstances may find different cognitive methodoogies effectively suitable to their particular condition is perfectly possible. But this global pluralism does not put any particular *individual* agent or group into a position of an indiscriminate indifferentism. Once their purposes and values are in place, the issue of pragmatic efficacy in *their* service becomes something fixed and determinate.

Since people are committed to a point of view, it is emphatically *not* a matter of rational indifference to them

---

[1] Stephen P. Stich, *The Fragmentation of Reason* (Cambridge, Mass., 1991), 158.

which alternative position is adopted. Given our status as creatures that have not only preferences but values, these cognitive issues will matter enormously to us and we defend them by elaborate arguments. Mere preferences, by contrast, are irrationalizable; they are what they are, without grounds or reasons. But values and standards—cognitive included—are always defensible. They can and must be supported by reasons and arguments that, to be sure, cannot themselves in the very nature of things be altogether value-free, but which nevertheless pivot on factors that are not *chosen* by us, but are situational *givens*.

6.3 *The Arbitrament of Experience*

The stance espoused throughout the present discussion has quite emphatically been that of a *perspectival rationalism* (or *contextualism*). Such a preferentialist position combines a pluralistic acknowledgement of distinct alternatives with a recognition that a sensible individual's choice among them is *not* rationally indifferent, but rather constrained by the probative indications of the *experience* that provides both the evidential basis and the evaluative criteria for effecting a rational choice.

In actual fact, after all, people who are confronted with a spectrum of competing alternatives are seldom altogether indifferent. Nor is it reasonable that they should be. For rational restraints to indifference are invariably imposed by a *context*. Such 'context' obtains at various, increasingly narrow levels:

1. humanity as such;
2. culture, civilization, tradition;
3. the transient practices and procedures adopted by parochial groups;
4. one's personal situation (i.e. character, disposition, idiosyncratic experience, etc.).

At each successive level of narrowing detail, increasingly specific contextual determinants of judgement and appraisal come into operation—factors that render it only normal, natural, and to be expected that people, being situated as they actually are, should adopt and implement a certain set of values, priorities, and beliefs. And it is clearly a demand of reason that different premises engender different conclusions, that different bases for reflection underwrite different thought constructions. Throughout, choice is never random or haphazard, but constrained and rationalized by the operation of those factors that define our situation as the particular individuals we are, where what makes for determination and specificity is the situational concreteness of a particular individual's particular experience. But such variation does not support an irrationalistic indifference—it itself is a demand of reason. That individuals who are differently situated in point of experience should arrive at different resolutions to their problems is not an argument for indifferentism but is a demand of rationality as such.

Even if we are pluralists and accept a wide variety of normative positions as being (abstractly speaking) available, still, if we have a doctrinal position at all—that is, if we are actually concerned for solving our cognitive and evaluative problems—we have no serious alternative to seeing our own positive as rationally superior. Faced with various possible answers to our questions, the sensible and appropriate course is clearly to figure out, as best one can, which one it is that deserves one's endorsement. But, of course, there is—or should be—a good rational basis for effecting such a choice, namely a normative perspective, whatever it be, that is based on the probative indications of our own experience. For there indeed is an objectifying impetus to avert our problem-resolutions from becoming a mere matter of indifferent choice based on arbitrary preferences. And throughout the sphere of rational inquiry this objectifying impetus lies in the appropriate utilization of the lessons of experience. Empiricism is our appropriate and optimal policy. We have to go on from where *we* are and proceed on the basis of our experential endowment. For us, a perspectival egalitarianism makes no sense in making our decisions regarding theoretical, practical, or evaluative matters.

A perspectival pluralism as such certainly does not underwrite any sort of arationalism. For recognizing that cognitive problems can admit of distinct solutions, each of which is optimal from a particular evaluative orientation, certainly does *not* mean that one should see the resolution here as a matter of rationally arbitrary choice—that one can simply pick at random because 'it makes no difference'. There is no universally appropriate diet, but that doesn't make it a matter of indifference what a person eats; there is no globally correct language, but that doesn't mean it is a matter of rational indifference how a particular person in a particular situation goes about communicating with others. None of these is a case of 'anything goes'. Context-relativization does *not* authorize arationalism.

The diversity at issue does not counterindicate rationality but rather exemplifies it. Even as different questions demand different answers in the rational nature of things, so different contexts demand different solutions. In these circumstances of sensitivity to context, diversity is not a barrier to rationality but an unavoidable demand of its operation.

To be sure, people's experience differs. Different individuals, different eras, different societies all have different bodies of experience. This being so, then where discordant thinkers are at issue is not *their* perspectival accommodation of their experience just as valid for them as ours is for us? No doubt, the answer here has to be affirmative. But it is an affirmative followed by an immediate: 'What of it?' The fact that someone else in a different position might conceivably be different is simply irrelevant *for us*.

For us, different positions in the experential order of things makes no difference whatsoever. We have to go on from where *we* are and proceed on the basis of our perspective. For us, a perspectival egalitarianism makes no sense. Indifferentism is ruled out by the fact that it is experience that is the determinative factor and for us, the experience at issue is *our* experience and cannot be someone else's.

The posture that emerges from this way of approaching the issue is thus that of a contextualistic rationalism:

Confronted with a pluralistic proliferation of alternatives you have your acceptance-determination methodology, and I have mine. Yours leads you to endorse P; mine leads me to endorse not-*P*. Yours is just as valid for you (in your methodology validity principles) as mine is for me. The situational differences of our contexts simply lead to different rational resolutions. And that's just the end of the matter.

The fact that the cognitive venture as a whole incorporates other positions does nothing to render a firm and fervent commitment to one's own position unjustifiable, let alone somehow improper and inappropriate.

6.4 *Some Possible Objections to an Empiricist Approach*

However, does this probative empiricism itself not engender indifferentism because any one person's body of experience is as valid as any other's—equally true and compelling? Yet 'equally true and compelling' for whom? The experiences of others certainly are not equivalent *for us*—save in so far as we somehow make them part and parcel of our own. For me, my own experience (vicarious experience included) is something unique—and uniquely compelling. You, to be sure, are in the same position—your experience is compelling, *for you*—but that's immaterial *to me*.

I have no choice but to proceed from whatever place fate has assigned me in the experiential scheme of things. (I cannot choose the time of my existence and only to a very limited extent its place.)

Cognitive or evaluative perspectives do not come to us *ex nihilo*. From the rational point of view such perspectives themselves require validation. And this process—with its focus on perspectival appropriateness—is itself something that is perspective presupposing. For, of course, we cannot assess the adequacy of a perspective in a vacuum, it must itself be supported from the position of a perspective of some sort. But in this world we are never totally bereft of such a basis: in the order of thought as in the world's physical order we always have a position of some sort. By the time one gets to the point of being able to think at all, there is always a background of available experience against which to form one's ideas. And just there is where one has to start. It is precisely because a certain position is appropriate *from where we stand* that makes this particular position of ours appropriate for us.

'But isn't such an experiential absolutism just relativism by another name—is it not itself just a relativism of a particular sort—an *experiential* relativism?' The answer lies in the consideration that whatever relativity there may be is a relativization to evidence, so that relativism's characteristic element of indifference is lacking. (It is just this, after all, that distinguishes indifferentist *relativism* form a rationalistic *contextualism*.) The point is that there is nothing *corrosive* about contextuality: it doesn't dissolve any of our commitments. Absolutism lies in the fact that, for us, our own experience is bound to be altogether compelling.

But does not a contextualistic pluralism put everyone's position on a par? Does it not underwrite the view that all the alternatives ultimately lie on the same level of acceptability? The question again is: Acceptable to whom? The 'life of the mind' as a whole maintains a certain Olympian indifference— a non-committal neutrality. However, this certainly does *not* mean that my position need be just as acceptable to you as to me. A sensible version of contextualistic pluralism will flatly refuse to put everyone's position on a par—save from the unachievable Olympian point of view of the community at large which is, of course, by its very nature unavailable to any single individual. For each individual stands fully and decidedly committed to his own orientation on the basis of his or her own experience, so that there is no question of a relativistic *indifferentism* in acknowledging the pivotal role of a cognitive perspective. A pluralism of contextually under-written cognitive positions does not lend to indifferentism precisely because a normative position is something that a valiant person cannot in the very nature of things view with indifference.

It makes no sense to take the line that all normative perspectives are equally acceptable, because where experiential bases of judgement are at issue, the pattern of our own experience is—for us at any rate—altogether decisive. After all, rationality requires that we attune our beliefs and evaluations to the overall pattern of our experience. For us, our own experience is rationally compelling. We could not (rationally) deviate from its dictates—and it would really make no sense for us to want to do so. We can no more separate from the indications of our own experience than we could separate ourselves from our own shadows. In sum, in so far as experience is indeed compelling one has to see an experiential pluralism as a context-defined rationalistic monism.

But is pluralism not a self-defeating position because it must take the view that all rivals to itself—absolutism, nihilism, and the rest—are just as meritorious? By no means! A sensible pluralism will not take such an egatilarian view at all. It will view those rivals as available, as deserving serious attention, perhaps even as plausible and tempting. But it will not—and need not—view them as correct, as sensible, or equal in merit with itself. It refuses to be dogmatic and to reject rival positions out of hand, without the courtesy of due scrutiny and evaluation. But it equally refuses to be gullible—to accept anything and everything on its own. It is open-minded, not empty-headed. It is certainly not monolothic and discriminatory in excluding all alternatives from the outset. But it is perfectly prepared to be preferential and discriminating in holding that our superior claims prevail in the final analysis. Its negative view of rivals is not unthinking and dogmatic but rests on a basis of reflection based on rational evaluation.[2]

6.5 *Pluralism is Compatible with Rational Commitment*

It is, in the eyes of some, a disadvantage of pluralism that it supposedly undermines one's commitment to one's own position. But this is simply fallacious. There is no good reason why a recognition that others, circumstanced as they are, are rationally entitled *in their circumstances* to hold a position at variance with ours should be construed to mean that we, *circumstanced as we are*, need feel any rational obligation to

---

[2] On the issues involved here see the discussion of open-minded versus dogmatic pluralism in Helmut Spinner, *Pluralismus als Erkenntnismodell* (Frankfurt am Main, 1974), 237–41.

abandon our position. In so far as one is rational (and no doubt not all of us are) one cannot see the alternatives as indifferent. Of course, different people have different interests, beliefs, obligations. But from the angle of rationality, I will (if indeed rational) have to take the line that in so far as a choice resolution is adequate for me it is also adequate for anyone in my experiential situation.

For the sake of clarity, one must distinguish between the standpoint of the individual and the standpoint of the group. Pluralistic diversity of opinion is a feature of the collective whole: it turns on the fact that different experiences engender different views. But from the standpoint of the individual this cuts no ice. We ourselves have no alternative to proceeding on the basis of what is available to us here and now. Granted, the group as a whole incorporates other alternatives, many or most of them incompatible with one's own. But the fact that the wider community as a whole contains other positions does nothing to render a firm and fervent commitment to one's own position somehow infeasible, let alone improper. We cannot rationally maintain a posture of indifference. Each thinker and every school of thought is bound to take a strongly negative stand toward its competitors: belittling their concerns, deploring their standards, downgrading their ideals, disliking their presuppositions, scorning their contentions, and so on. To accept the sort of relativism at issue in a rational indifferentism is to take a position that is unsustainable and indeed in the final analysis indefensible.

As long as we are *serious* about rational inquiry we must actually have a perspective of consideration and take an evaluative position by assuming a normative-value orientation. And here—'internally' from our own point of orientation—we ourselves simply cannot consider other positions as genuinely on a par with our own in point of merit. As long as we have 'the courage of our convictions'—as long as we stand committed to the cognitive values that undergird our cognitive position—we are led preferentially to their own logical conclusion. Once a probative orientation is seriously adopted and its standards of assessment are in place only one 'correct' answer will generally be available.

Recognizing that others see some matter differently from

ourselves need not daunt us in attachment to our own views. It may give us second thoughts—may invite us to rethink— but it has no real bearing on the *outcome* of such reflections. There is, after all, no conflict if a variant experiential perspective leads others to see the true or the right differently from ourselves. Given that—*ex hypothesi*—we ourselves do indeed occupy our perspective, we are, of course, bound to see *our* truth as the truth, although we nevertheless can and do recognize that others see the matter in a different light.

After all, we ourselves are bound to see our own (rationally adopted) standards as superior to the available alternatives— and are, presumably, rationally entitled to do so in the light of the cognitive values we ourselves endorse. Rational is as rational does—it hinges on the norms, standards, and criteria that we ourselves can endorse as rationally appropriate on the basis of a well-considered view as to what is appropriate for anybody. Admittedly, the rationally appropriate exploitation of their differential experiences is bound to lead rational inquirers in different directions. But one can certainly combine acknowledgement of a contextualistic pluralism of possible alternatives with a firm and dedicated commitment to the standards intrinsic to one's own position.

Nothing in perspectival pluralism as such compels us to see our cognitive commitments as *mere opinions*. They are indeed opinions of sorts, but there is nothing 'mere' about them. They are *judgements*—matters of reasoned conviction for whose acceptance we (warrantedly) take ourselves to have good reasons. The fact that these 'good reasons' can only count as good from the perspective of a given cognitive-value orientation nowise precludes them from being good reasons.

The key lesson is that one must take a stand. One must 'choose sides' in the debate: 'Never mind about the others; they may follow a different drummer. Our job is to follow ours'. In the very nature of the case, we have no alternative to proceeding on this basis. If we give up on the pursuit of *our truth*, we give up on the pursuit of *the truth* itself, seeing that we can only get at the truth through the mediation of our ideas about it.

An experiential pluralism of cognitive orientations is thus no impediment to doctrinal commitment. There is no reason that the mere existence of different views and positions should leave us immobilized like the ass of Buridan between the alternatives. Nor are we left with the grey emptiness of egalitarianism that looks to all sides with neutrality and uncommitted indifference. It makes a crucial difference to everybody which position one adopts, though not in exactly the same way. We cannot view doctrinal disagreement in the light of a 'mere divergence of opinion'. It is a serious conflict— as one would expect when something as important as one's values comes into play. Each inquirer—each school of thought—is bound to see its own rationally espoused position as rationally appropriate. An acknowledgement of pluralism is no invitation to abandoning one's dedication to one's own position.

We not only have an *epistemic* justification to stick by our own opinions, we have in various circumstances a *moral duty* to do so. Such a situation arises whenever the best interests of third parties are involved. To return to an example already mentioned above, if someone lies ill and unconscious in the street and you propose forming a circle to say incantations, then I, persuaded that summoning a doctor is the thing to do, would be acting in a morally reprehensible way if I acceded to your view of the matter in the interests of consensus.

But does this idea of an 'entitlement to one's own position' not condemn one to parochialism? Does it not mean that inquirers are simply limited to addressing the like-minded?

By no means! The aim and intent of the cognitive enterprise is strictly universal. Yet the unavoidable fact is that reality is going to frustrate the realization of this aspiration. The reality of the situation is that only the like-minded will accept one's ideas and in the way in which one intends—in epistemic, evaluative, or practical matters, only a limited constituency will be sympathetic. But this is a fact of life regarding rational procedure which has no negative bearing on the validity of its deliverances. It means no more than that differently situated people must resolve their problems differently—which, after all is not an invalidation of reason but one of its requirements.

To acknowledge that other people hold views different from ours, and to concede the prospect that we may, even in the end, simply be unable to win them over by rational suasion, is emphatically not to accept an indifferentism to the effect that their views are just as valid or correct as ours are. To acquiesce in a situation where others think differently from oneself is neither to endorse their views not to abandon one's own. In many departments of life—in matters of politics, philosophy, art, morality, and so on—we certainly do not take the position that the correctness of our own views is somehow undermined and their tenability compromised by the circumstance that others do not share them. And there is no good reason why we should see the issue all that differently in matters of inquiry or evaluation.

A sensible pluralist acknowledges not only that different people (groups or schools of thought) have different standards, but that they can do so appropriately given their differential emplacement in the cognitive scheme of things. But of course it does not follow from this that the pluralist need be disloyal to his own standards (any more than it follows that my acknowledging your spouse to be appropriate *for you* constitutes on my part an act of disloyalty towards my own).

If we are going to be rational we must take—and have no choice but to take—the stance that our own standards (of truth, value, and choice) are the appropriate ones. Be it in employing or in evaluating them, we ourselves must see our own standards as definitive because just exactly this is what it is for them to *be* our own standards—their being our standards *consists in our seeing them in this light*. To insist that we are not entitled to view our standards as definitive would be to prevent our having standards at all. We have to see our standards in an absolutistic light—as the uniquely right appropriately valid ones—because exactly this is what is at issue in their being our standards of authentic truth, value, or whatever. And of course those who would deny us this right—who say that we are not entitled to adopt those standards of ours—do no more than insist that it is by *their* standards (who else's?) inappropriate for us to have these standards, and thus are simply pitting their standards against ours. To insist that we should view our standards with indifference is to deny us the prospects of having any standards at all. Commitment at this level is simply unavoidable. Our cognitive or evaluative perspective would not be our perspective did we not deem it rationally superior to others.

Once we have done our rational best to substantiate our position, the mere existence of alternatives need give us no pause. The avoidance of responsibility lies in an indifferentism that sees merit everywhere and validity nowhere (or vice versa), thereby relieving us of any and all duty to investigate the issues in a serious, workmanlike way. We are diven back to the view of the pre-Platonic Sophists, who maintained that with respect to the great issues of human concern something is to be said on all sides and that in consequence there is no such thing as a true position. To take this stance is indeed possible—but not without abandoning responsibilities as an inquirer.

People incline to object along the following lines against a downgrading of consensus:

> To acquiesce in disagreement and regard dissensus as a state of affairs that is not only actual but even *tolerable* is to become a relativist—to see others as equally entitled to *their* view of the truth as we are to *ours*. And then we are no longer in a position to see our own convictions as the authentically correct version of the truth—so that our commitment to attaining the truth is seriously undermined.

Plausible though it may sound, this objection is profoundly wrong. Dissensus-tolerance does *not* entail an indifferentist relativism. For one thing, it is perfectly compatible with an acceptance of *global* dissensus that certain *local* particular issues can be settled with universal agreement. (No scientist denies that lead is heavier than copper.) For another thing, even where there is disagreement, there may well nevertheless be (and indeed often is) general agreement on the idea that further investigations conducted in the future will settle the issue decisively one way or another. But these qualifications do not alter the basic situation of dissensus as a fact of life.

Jean Paul Sartre deplored the attempt to secure rationally validated knowledge, which he saw as a way of avoiding responsibility for *making* something of oneself, for 'choosing one's own project', seeing that the real truth is not something one can make up as one goes along but is something one regards as entitled to one's recognition (to a subordination of sorts on one's part). But this view turns the matter topsy-turvy. Not the pursuit of truth but its *abandonment* represents a failure of nerve and a crisis of confidence.

There is nothing admirable in the currently fashionable inclination to doctrinal detachment with its concomitant reluctance to trust one's personal judgement in matters of human significance. Indifferentism betokens a manifestly wishy-washy unwillingness to adopt a position, to stand up and be counted. It represents a regrettable unpreparedness to take intellectual responsibility—to say: 'I've investigated the matter as best I can, and this is the result at which I've arrived. Here I stand, I can do no other. If you wish to stand with me, then welcome to you; if not, then I shall view the fact of your disagreement with resigned indifference until such time as somebody can convince me that my position is untenable.'

The deliberations of this chapter—and the central thesis of this book—may accordingly be summarized as follows. An individual need not be intimidated by the fact of disagreement—it makes perfectly good sense for people to do their rational best towards securing evidentiated beliefs and justifiable choices without undue worry about whether or not others disagree. And it is fallacious to insist on a quest for consensus on the grounds that dissensus and pluralism are rationally intolerable. A community that exhibits and accepts internal disagreements is in principle perfectly viable—it makes perfectly good sense for a society to refrain from seeking to constrain agreement in matters of opinion, valuation, and choice, and to let a productive rivalry of discord prevail within communally manageable and excess-avoiding limits.

A perspectivally differentiated position is (or should be) good enough for sensible individuals—precisely because that position-determinative perspective of ours is by hypothesis *our* perspective. And for groups, a sensibly restrained situation of dissensual pluralism should prove not only acceptable but even (within limits) advantageous—not only because the stimulus of rivalry can provide the goad to progress, but also because a benevolent acquiescence in differences helps the community to flourish, and because an other-respecting spirit of live-and-let-live is inherently benign and productive. There is nothing rationally mandatory about the quest for consensus.

7

Problems of Evaluative Consensus

7.1 *Consensus and Evaluative Norms*

The preceding chapters have focused their critique upon the issue of *cognitive* consensus matters of knowledge and belief. We now turn rather more briefly to a consideration of *axiological* consensus in matters of priorities and values.

The ancient Sophists, Hobbes and his followers, and the Scottish moralists of the eighteenth century, all believed that normative matters—moral issues included—rooted in consensus. Value and virtue, so they taught, are ultimately conventional, bringing on people's agreeing to adopt a common viewpoint with agreed standards of preferability and worth.[1] But can consensus in and of itself suffice to establish evaluative norms? John Stuart Mill apparently thought so when he wrote:

The only proof capable of being given that an object is visible, is that people actually see it. The only proof that a sound is audible, is that people hear it: and so of the other sources of our experience. In like manner, I apprehend, the sole evidence it is possible to produce that anything is desirable, is that people do actually desire it . . . No reason can be given why the general happiness is desirable, except that each person, so far as he believes it to be attainable, desires his own happiness.[2]

For Mill, the fact of people's agreeing in desiring something suffices to validate its normative desirability. But critics of this

---

[1] For the Sophists see G. B. Kerferd, *The Sophists* (Cambridge, 1981); for Hobbes and his followers see Gregory Kavka, *Hobbesian Moral and Political Theory* (Princeton, NJ, 1986); for the Scotsmen see V. M. Hope, *Virtue by Consensus* (Oxford, 1989).

[2] J. S. Mill, *Utilitarianism* (London, 1859), ch. 4.

conception of Mill's have been so numerous and effective that the argument at issue has earned for itself the name of 'Mill's fallacy'. For (so it is held) in inferring normative desirability from factually being desired, the argument confuses '*able* to be desired' with '*deserving* of being desired'. And, after all, the circumstance that people actually desire something, while it indeed shows that this item *can* be desired, no more shows that it is *deserving* of being desired than does the fact that people actually admire someone establish that this person is really *worthy* of admiration.

The critique at issue was in essence already deployed by Socrates against Protagoras in the account given in Plato's dialogue *Theaetetus*. For here Socrates presses the following question:

> If some ordinary man thinks he is going to take a fever . . . and a physician thinks the contrary, whose opinion shall we expect the future to prove right? . . . [And] in regard to the sweetness or dryness which will be in a wine, is it not the opinion of the winegrower rather than that of the lyre-player that will be valid?[3]

The implication is clear: what people actually think is one thing and what deserves to be thought—what people *should* think—is something very different, something an expert is in a far better position to judge. And so, Socrates insists, the fact that people *think* that something is advantageous for them does not mean that they are necessarily right—that it *actually is* advantageous for them. And similarly the fact that people *think* that something is desirable does not mean that it actually *is* so.

The crux of such a critique is that the argument

People desire X
_____
Therefore: People ought to have X

simply does not work. To make such an argument work we would need to add a premiss about the value of the item at issue. Thus, for example, the argument

People desire X
X is inherently a good thing for people to have
_____
Therefore: people ought to have X

[3] *Theaetetus* 178c.

is perfectly cogent. But of course it is that second premiss that does all the work here in going beyond the mere fact of its being desired into the normative nature of the item itself.

To be sure, that second pivotal premiss can be weakened somewhat without undue damage to the argumentation. After all, the inference

People want X
There is no reason to think that X is a bad thing
_____
Therefore: People ought to have X

is still perfectly cogent. For what assures its cogency is a

Principle of Benevolence. A world in which people have what they want is a better world than one in which they do not, provided there is no harm to what they want (i.e. no harm to them or to others or to the world's normative nature of things).

Given such a Principle of Benevolence, the 'mere fact' of consensuality (in point of something's being desired) is evidentially sufficient to establish a norm (as point of desirability). For this principle underwrites the further thesis:

When there is no reason to think that what people want is harmful, then they ought (ideally) to have it

And *this* principle, together with the premisses of the preceding argument, suffices to underwrite that argument's conclusion. These considerations indicate not only (and trivially) that what people want is *desired* by them, but also the more substantial conclusion that it is (in the absence of counter-indications) *desirable* for them to have it. The crux of Mill's inference from being desired to being desirable is in fact that is implicit in the cognate benevolence principle:

Something is established as a *prima-facie* desideratum by the mere fact of being generally desired, i.e. by the fact (when fact it is) that people want it.

To be sure the factually desired is not a desideratum pure and simple but only a *prima-facie* desideratum—i.e. something that can be maintained as a desideratum only under the premiss that it is not inherently problematic (i.e. not by nature something negative).

Accordingly, what is at issue in Mill's argumentation—on a generous construction of the matter—is an *enthymeme* in which the Principle of Benevolence and a supposition about the innocuous nature of the item at issue combine to underwrite a perfectly cogent course of reasoning. Consensus in the matter of desiring something indeed is sufficient to establish *prima-facie* desirability. Given the Principle of Benevolence, the 'mere fact' of consensuality (in point of being desired) may be seen as *evidentially* sufficient to establish a norm (as point of desirability). The argumentation of 'Mill's fallacy' is—to re-emphasize—not a *fallacy* at all, but an *enthymeme*, and a rather plausible-looking one at that.

But just how plausible? We are obviously to take the benevolent line that it is a good thing for people—taken at the collective level—to get what they want in so far as they can agree in this matter of wanting. Yet this is where the problem lies. For in the final analysis the move to desirability from being desired—to value from being valued—can never go entirely unmediated. Some reference to appropriateness is required—some (deeply normative) assumption or presumption that the people at issue are being rational—that what they *do* value is *worth* valuing, that they are not swept away (individually or as a group) by some inherently defective (absurd, foolish) approach to the business of evaluation. If value as such lay in the eyes of its beholders, the question of appropriateness could not arise. But the fact is that it is always and unavoidably there.

7.2 *The Issue of Axiological Consensus: Value Diversity and the Key Role of Experience*

Is it not simply fortuitous that different people should have different values? Should there not in the end be an agreed uniformity of evaluation that embraces all rational agents? Furthermore, are value orientations rationally grounded or are they little more than arbitrary and fortuitous attitudes? A cluster of important issues lurks here.

Hume was right in this, at any rate: values are derivable neither from considerations of abstract reason nor from considerations of observed fact. The reality of it is that the value domain is self-contained—one cannot enter into it from without. All values, cognitive ones included, involve an orientation towards decision and action, thus incorporating an element of position-taking that can only be justified on a normative basis of some sort.[4]

The diversity of values is inherent in the fact that *homo sapiens* is not a mere mechanism. Our emplacement in nature is sufficiently context-variable to permit diverse responses to uniform situations. For our valuations are bound to reflect not the present circumstances alone, but the course of one's formative past experience as well. To be a person is to be a creature that can to some extent shape its own set of priorities and values independently of others on the basis of its own probative course of experience.

Values compete and conflict—and people's ideas about them do so as well. They do not turn on the passive observation of impersonal facts, but inhere in an active engagement in the world's affairs. They do not issue from intersubjectively invariant considerations, but emerge as products of reflective human judgement based on individual differences and variations of needs and wants. There is, clearly, a wide variety of discrepant and ultimately incommensurable value positions, seeing that your lifestyle may require prioritizing A over B and mine B over A. And given such a value-pluralism, it is only normal, natural, and to be expected that different people—given their differences in individual make-up, personal experience, and social context—should arrive at different commitments and priorities among them.[5]

Value disagreement is not only fundamental but also ineliminable. Different people have different values and priorities and accordingly evaluate the available alternatives

---

[4] It should be stressed that this thesis does not call for postulating an absolute fact–value divide, maintaining that facts are entirely *irrelevant* to values. All that need be maintained for its substantiation is that factual considerations by themselves leave value issues to some extent underdetermined. The relevant issues are examined in some detail in ch. 3, 'How Wide is the Gap Between Facts and Values?', in the author's *Baffling Phenomena* (Totowa, NJ, 1991).

[5] For an illuminating discussion of the complex issues relevant here see John Kekes's insightful study of *The Morality of Pluralism* (Princeton, NJ, 1993).

differently. And these conflicting evaluations are not, in general, capable of compromise: we cannot split the difference. Variability is built into values because *value judgements are defined as such relative to one another.* To give X priority over Y is sensible only in a context where the prospect of giving Y priority over X also beckons. A value position can exist as such only in the context of inherent contrast with rival alternatives.

As long as people think themselves to have good reason for prizing things differently—for making different assessments in point of value, significance, importance, and the like—that is, so long as people are *people*, beings with a value-structure of their own, consensus, however attractive in the abstract, is not in the concrete a practicable or even desirable state of affairs. A fundamental variability of reflective evaluations in point of values, ideals, aims, and aspirations prevails among people, engendering a pluralism in cognitive, practical, doctrinal, and even political regards.[6] In sum, value dissensus inheres in the human condition.

7.3 *Is Evaluative Disagreement Irrational?*

People have different values. But is it *reasonable* for them to do so? After all, the impetus of reason is, as we have seen, universal: the principles of rationality hold good for everyone alike.

To deal with this issue sensibly, it helps to distinguish the principles themselves from their variable implementations in different contexts. For no doubt the sorts of consideration that make it *reasonable* for a particular person—given his or her particular situation and circumstances—to hold a certain set of values are something impersonal and universal. (Anyone— even the most affluent millionaire—can readily understand why someone who lives in straightened circumstances should be mindful of even small expenditures.) Those high-level evaluative determinations at issue in rationality itself are universal. But where civilized people do—or should—agree

---

[6] Regarding philosophical pluralism and its ramifications, see the collection of interesting essays gathered in the *Monist*, 73 (July 1990).

about generic values (the value of human life, as such, for example, or of people's physical and emotional well-being) they may—and properly can—disagree about its implementation (where a human life begins, for example, or under what conditions a human life has ceased to be such and declined into mere biological existence). Even where we can reach (or demand) consensus on abstract and general desiderata, this need not extend all that far along the descent to concreteness. The prospect of variation—and thus disagreement—in matters of evaluation is inherent in the human condition, reflecting the differences among differently constituted and differently situated individuals. When applied to different situations those uniform considerations yield different results. In rational valuation even as in rational cognition, the universality of determinative principles does not make for a universality of concrete determinations.

Our values emerge from the operation of many different factors: our culture, the 'spirit of the times', the influence of our teachers and their opponents, our general intellectual heritage and orientation, and so on. Conditioning experiences of every kind—forged under the pressure of nature and nurture, of personal temperament, economic and social settings, cultural traditions, etc.—will all come into it. A person's values reflect a diversified spectrum of conceptual and causal determinants. For better or worse, people have different values both because of differences in needs and wants, and because the experiences on which human values hinge are substantially variable across the spectrum of the human community. Rationally adopted values, like rationally adopted beliefs, must reflect the structure of an agent's experiences, and these are bound to differ among differently situated individuals. Such a view of inquiry envisages a kind of enlarged empiricism. Empiricists see cognitive diversity as ultimately rooted in the diversity of *sensory* experience, whereas what is presently at issue is a diversity of *affective* experience. People's value postures are the product of a complex interaction between nature and nurture, with both of these factors playing a key role. Nature (natural inclinations, preferences, biases) makes a substantial impact. And nurture, represented by a course of experience under the conditioning impetus of cultural setting, historical context, and so on, is even more important. Since different courses of experience are incompossible realities, the variation of values within the wider community is effectively inevitable; experience is too diversified and variegated in philosophically relevant situations to issue in a single value scheme.

The long and short of it is that a demand for value consensus is unrealistic and unreasonable. Evaluative disagreement is not only pervasive but is in fact rationally inevitable because rational people's values are bound to reflect their circumstantially conditioned experiences, and circumstances differ. Accordingly, the impersonal universality of the principles of reason does not mean that an evaluative consensus can be expected—or demanded.

The Habermas–Apel approach to evaluative consensuality seeks to close the is–ought gap by briding over the fact–value divide in trying to exploit certain supposedly inevitable ground rules of successful communication as a basis for extracting the basic principles of ethics, moving from what is needed for an effective informative discussion to validating the ground rules of moral interaction in general.[7] Its basic strategy is to extract the realization of an evaluative (and specifically moral) consensus from the mechanisms for achieving an informative (informationally factual) consensus. The decisive difficulty here lies in the move from effectiveness to obligation—from 'here is what needs to be done for the realization of a communicative consensus' to 'here is what should be done on moral grounds'. But there is a great gap here. The fact is that a consensus can effectively issue from bad as well as good motives and can altogether lack a morally appropriate basis. Only if we put a normatively positive sort of consensuality-promotion into consensus formation—as Habermas in fact ultimately does—can we obtain an evaluatively meritorious sort of process and procedure. And from the value point of view such a process is clearly circular: we

---

[7] See Jürgen Habermas, *Theorie des kommunikativen Handelns* (Frankfurt am Main, 1981), and Karl-Otto Apel, 'Fallibilismus, Konsenztheorie der Wahrheit und Letztbegründung', in H. Schnädelbach (ed.), *Philosophie und Begründung* (Frankfurt am Main, 1987).

get morality out of consensuality considerations only because we packed it into them in the first place.

7.4 *Cognitive Ramifications of Value Disagreement*

Evaluative disagreement is basic to disagreement in general. Even factual disagreement generally roots in evaluative conflicts, arising when different parties apply different norms and standards to the evaluation of evidence, and thus bring different *cognitive* values to bear.

Cognitive valuation calls for *according significance* to certain considerations, seeing certain matters as important, and taking certain cases to be archetypical—or at least highly relevant. Such cognitive values involve taking a particular approach to determining the bearing of 'the objective facts', and indicate an evaluative response to an objective situation.

Whether a (perfectly rational) person regards a certain body of relevant information as 'sufficient' to entitle us to answer a question depends not on the abstract logic of the situation alone, but also upon (1) how urgent and important it is, given his or her situation, to have an answer to the question at all, and (2) how risk-aversive he or she is in assessing the gravity and seriousness of a possible error. Not 'the mere facts' alone but our particular relationship to them can (quite appropriately) influence our cognitive and evaluative decision-making. In this influencing of our problem-solving endeavours these factors will also influence the conclusions and infer-ences we draw from further relevant information. And, of course, given the variation of individuals and groups in this regard, it is only normal, natural, and to be expected that different individuals and groups will—with complete rational appropriateness—hold different sorts of views on the issues.

Inquiry is a fundamentally reflective enterprise. And what it pre-eminently reflects is the structure of human experience. As experience changes (as between different people or between the different temporal stages of a person's life) so do values change, and changes in cognitive values bring changes in personal judgement in their wake. There is no prospect of uniformity, of consensus. The biblical story of the Tower of

Babel carries a far-reaching lesson. For better or worse, the prospect of homogeneous uniformity across the human scene is unattainable. The imparticularity of evaluative consensus carries that of cognitive consensus in its wake.

7.5 *Is Value Disagreement Communally Incapacitating?*

Does the fact that their evaluations cannot be blended, or compounded, or combined mean that a group of evaluatively disagreeing individuals cannot reach accommodation in a collectively acceptable position?

It is by no means necessary that a pluralistic society in which various subgroups have different values and priorities should find itself hamstrung in the process of collective decision. Evaluative disagreement is not socially incapacitating because agreement in practical measures does *not* require or presuppose evaluative agreement. For people can agree that alternative A is preferable to alternative B even where their evaluative grounding for this conclusion is radically different. Moreover, in a situation of value pluralism the choice is not one between blandness and warfare—many forms of barter and compromise always exist, no doubt varying with the specific characteristics of particular cases. When you value X more than I do, and I value Y more than you do, the process of accommodation between us—with me giving up some X and you some Y—becomes a practicable and potentially attractive pathway to conflict-avoidance. Not only is a disagreement in valuation not necessarily socially incapacitating, but it can—in suitable circumstances—even provide a basis on which various sorts of generally productive collaboration can be founded. The unachievability of evaluative consensus need not and should not be an obstacle to constructive communal coexistence in a well-ordered society. Indeed one of the characterizing hallmarks of a well-oriented society turns on the extent to which it makes communal concert and co-operation possible notwithstanding its members' disagreement on evaluative matters, enabling people to live and labour together in peace and harmony, their different evaluative orientations notwithstanding.

8

Does Communication Require Consensus?

8.1 *Is Communication Predicated on Consensus?*

Does communication require consensus? Is successful communicative contact among people predicated on their having a body of shared beliefs regarding the matters at issue? Many writers certainly think so, reasoning somewhat as follows: 'We cannot possibly convey information to one another unless we agree, at the very least, about the terms at issue. For how can I impart my views about rabbits to you unless you understand by "rabbits" exactly what I understand by the term?' But plausible though it may sound, this view of the matter has its problems.

In a recent discussion of the topic one reads:

It is clear that the meaning, grammar, and reference of language is, in some sense, determined by implicit consensus . . . [To be sure, in the case of] a technical word like 'molecule' . . . the question of whether certain objects are or are not molecules is decided by appeal to physical scientists . . . [And] here the consensus over usage presupposes a consensus about who is authoritative, who is expert, in the use and application of the words in question.[1]

But in *this* context it is a bit strange to speak of a 'consensus'— be it explicit or tacit. The fact that people adopt certain linguistic practices—and co-ordinate their language use—is scarcely a matter of *consensus*: they do not somehow come to

---

[1] Keith Lehrer and Carl Wagner, *Rational Consensus in Science and Society* (Dordrecht, 1990), 12.

agree that 'cat' means cat: they just learn how the language works. Learning how language works or learning how a typewriter works—or, for that matter, how to play golf—is a matter of mastering a certain sort of skill. And skills or competencies of this sort, whether solitary or interactive, are hardly matters of *consensus*—agreement simply does not enter into it; it is a matter of 'learning how the thing is done', how to 'play the game'. Language mastery consists in acquiring a capacity for the conduct of communicative interactions rather than counting the entry into an agreement of some sort: like dancing, it calls for *co-ordination* rather than *agreement*.

Let us probe more deeply into the roots of the matter, focusing our discussion on the issue of *reference*.

8.2 *The Communicative Dispensability of Common Conception*

In the fifth century BC, Anaximander of Miletus doubtless made many correct contentions about the sun—for example, that it is not a mass of burning material pulled about on its circuit through the heavens by a deity driving a chariot drawn by a winged horse. But Anaximander's *conception* of the sun (as a hole in the firmament through which one can see the cosmic fire encircling the world) was seriously wrong. The sun, as he conceived and discussed it, is something drastically different from the sun as it is by *our* lights. A commonality of belief on this particular issue is notable by its absence. But this does not preclude us from understanding what he was talking about.

This points to a crucial reflection: our conception of any real particular, be it the sun or yon maple tree, is always held tentatively, subject to a mental reservation of sorts, in that we maintain a full recognition that this conception of ours may ultimately prove to be mistaken. Our use of language is undergirded by the fact that we view conceptions as inherently defeasible and fallible. For having a correct conception of something as the object it is requires that we have all the important facts about it right—that our ideas are in substantial agreement with the facts of the matter. And since the prospect of discovering further important facts (let alone errors in our beliefs) can never be eliminated, the possibility can never be ruled out that matters may so eventuate that we ultimately (with the wisdom of hindsight) acknowledge the impropriety of our earlier conceptions. Thus with *conceptions*—unlike propositions or *contentions*—incompleteness always makes for some element of inadequacy. A conception that is based on incomplete data is thereby deficient and will for this very reason be at least partially incorrect. To be sure, an inadequate or incomplete *description* of anything is not thereby false—the statements we make about it may be perfectly true as far as they go. But an inadequate or incomplete *conception* of a thing is thereby one that we have no choice but to presume to be incorrect as well, seeing that where there is incompleteness we cannot justifiably take the stance that it relates only to inconsequential matters and touches nothing important. Accordingly, our conceptions of particular things are always to be viewed not just as cognitively *open-ended*, but also as *corrigible*, and this holds not just for particulars but for matters of generality as well.

In his *Cartesian Meditations*, Edmund Husserl developed the interesting idea of a *horizon* in perceptual knowledge, a phenomenon that roots in the fact that our awareness always pertains to a mere *aspect or part* of the object that we actually perceive, and never the whole thing. It follows that some element of incompleteness, and thus of indeterminacy, is present throughout perceptual knowledge, because the percipient can never be sure that, for all that he knows, the unperceived aspects of the object may be quite different from what he or she *thinks* them to be. Our conceptualized knowledge of things is always limited by a horizon across which we cannot 'see' and beyond which matters are so situated that the impressions we have based upon our incomplete information may well prove false. The very idea of a *thing* that lies at the basis of our discourse about the things of this world is thus based on a certain sort of tentativity and fallibilism—the implicit recognition that our own personal or even communal conception of things may well be incorrect, and is in any case inadequate. At the bottom of our thought about things there is always a certain wary scepticism that recognizes the possibility of error. And this fact has important implications for the business of communication. For it means that the idea that in order to understand a speaker the hearer must agree with this speaker's conception of the matter is gravely mistaken. I need not think about rabbits as you do to talk with you about them.

Admittedly our ventures in communication proceed against the background of a hope that agreement can be reached. And the possibility of agreement is, no doubt, a presupposition of the venture—the idea of reaching a meeting of minds always hovers in the background. But of course such *possibilities* are frail reeds indeed, incapable of supporting anything of substance. (If I *look for* something—the source of a certain sound, say—I doubtless suppose that it is something I will be able to see. But this of course tells me effectively zero about what this sound-source will look like.)

Throughout the context of communication about particular things, no claim is made for the *primacy* of our conceptions, or for the *correctness* of our conceptions, or even for the mere *agreement* of our conceptions with those of others. Conceptions indeed are secondary and largely irrelevant. It is the fundamental intention to discuss 'the thing itself' that predominates and overrides any mere dealing with the thing as we ourselves conceive of it.

This ever-operative contrast between a person-indifferent 'the thing itself' and 'the thing as we ourselves take it to be' means that we are never in a position to attribute definitive finality to our conception of a thing. We are never entitled to claim to have exhausted it *au fond* in cognitive regards—that we have managed to effect its complete capture within our epistemic grasp. For to make this claim would, in effect, be to *identify* 'the thing itself' in terms of 'our own conception of it', an identification which would effectively remove the former item (the thing itself) from the stage of public consideration as an independent entity in its own right by endowing our conception with decisively determinative force.

Our concept of a *real thing* as a commonly available focus is accordingly a fixed point, a shared and stable centre around which communication revolves, the invariant focus of potentially diverse conceptions. What is to be determinative, decisive, definitive (etc.) of the things at issue in my discourse is not my conception, or yours, or indeed anyone's conception at all. The conventionalized intention discussed above means that a co-ordination of conceptions is nowise requisite for the possibility of communication: your statements about a thing will convey something to me even if my conception of it is altogether different from yours. To derive informative benefit from the declarations of others, we need not take ourselves to share *views* of the world, but only to take the stance that we share *the world* being discussed. The crux is a determination of ours to use whatever fair and reasonable means we can to derive the benefits of communication with others, affording them informative clues about our thinking and deriving from theirs what we can—if need be by way of conjecture and interpretation.

Seen in *this* light, the key point may be put as follows: It is indeed a presupposition of successful communication in matters of information-transmission that we purport (that is, claim and intend) to make true statements about the objective things at issue. But it is *not* required for such discourse that we have (or even purport to have) an adequate, let alone true, subjective conception of these things. On the contrary, we must deliberately abstain from staking any claim that our own conceptions are definitive if we are to engage successfully in discourse. We deliberately put the whole matter of conception aside—abstracting from the question of the agreement of my conception with yours, and all the more from the issue of which of us has the right conception. And in putting the correctness of conceptions aside we also put aside the entire issue of agreement and consensus. Their conception of things simply need not be correct by our lights.

The fact that communication is not predicated on agreement in regard to the conceptions of things means, *a fortiori*, that we need not be correct in our conceptions of things to communicate successfully about them. This points, in part, to the important fact that I need not agree with what you are saying to understand you. But it points also, and even more importantly, to the consideration that my having a conception of a thing massively different from yours will not prevent me from taking you to be talking about the same thing that I have in mind. Objectivity and referential commonality of focus are matters of initial presumption or presupposition. The issue here is not with what *is* understood, but with what *is to be* understood (by anybody) in terms of certain generalized and communicative intentions. (The issue here is not one of *meaning* but only of *meaningfulness*.)

To be sure, it is sometimes said that to understand other people's discourse we must agree with them, must share their beliefs.[2] But this is simply wrong. To understand others we may need to know (or conjecture) what their beliefs are, but we need certainly not *agree* with them. We can understand what Galen says about the four humours or what Leibniz says about his windowless monads without agreeing with these writers as to the issues involved.

But is not a consensus of sorts built into the fact that successful communication requires common terms of reference? If we are going to talk together about forks, don't we have to have a consensus about what 'forks' are? Not necessarily. To begin with, it is not *agreement* but common (i.e. shared) *custom* that is constitutive of 'correct usage'. And, more importantly, we need not share conceptions to communicate. I can make perfectly good use of someone's fork talk without agreeing with their conceptions as to what forks are all about. To draw communicative benefit from *their* (the declarers') declarations, we (the recipients) must invest a certain amount of effort and risk in the venture. Proceeding with a determination to extract information, we must undertake various suppositions and presumptions with respect to their communicative practices. If the situation is such that I know (or have excellent evidence to believe) that by 'fork' Smith understands what I mean by 'spoon', then I shall not be prevented from figuring out what he is saying. Again, whereas I myself believe forks are eating implements, if I know (or have excellent reason to believe) that *Y* thinks of them as screw-sorters, then I shall have no difficulty grasping what he says about them. Communication requires some *understanding* of meanings, but not an *agreement* about them. It roots in *interpretation*, but the impetus to some sort of

[2] See e.g. Donald Davidson, 'On the Very Idea of a Conceptual Scheme', *Proceedings and Addresses of the American Philosophical Association*, 47 (1973–4), 5–20. And cf. the critique of this position in ch. 2, 'Conceptual Schemes', of the author's *Empirical Inquiry* (Totowa, NJ, 1982), 27–60.

consilience or endorsement is not essential to it. A determination to grasp ideas and concepts is required, but an *acceptance* of beliefs is nowise essential. The sort of co-ordination that communication requires is not a matter of consensus.

8.3 *The Presumption of Communicative Intent*

In our communication regarding things we must be able to exchange information with our contemporaries and to transmit information to our successors. And we must be in a position to do this in the face of the presumption that *their* conceptions of things are not only radically different from *ours*, but conceivably also rightly different. What is at issue here is not the commonplace that we do not know *everything* about anything. Rather, the key consideration is the more interesting thesis that it is a crucial precondition of the possibility of successful communication about things that we must avoid laying any claim either *to the completeness or even to the ultimate correctness of our own conceptions* of the things at issue. Communication is too important to be put at the mercy of consensus—let alone correctness.

Any pretentions to the predominance, let alone to the correctness, of our own conceptions regarding the world's furniture must be put aside in communicative situations. Rather, what is crucial is the fundamental intention to deal with the interpersonally accessible things of the objective order of this 'real world'. If our assertoric commitments did not transcend the specific information that we ourselves have on hand, then any endeavour to 'get in touch' with others about a shared objective world would face grave, indeed, virtually insuperable obstacles.

This postulated (or presumed) intention to take real objects to be at issue, objects as they are in themselves, with our potentially idiosyncratic conceptions of them acknowledged but put aside, is fundamental to communication. For without this conventionalized intention we should not be able to convey information—or misinformation—to one another about a shared 'objective' world. We could not practicably establish communicative contact about a common objective item of discussion if our discourse were geared inseparably to things conceived of in terms of *our own* specific information about them. For if we were to set up our own conception as somehow definitive and decisive, then we would at once erect a grave impediment to the prospect of successful communication with one another. For communication could then only proceed retrospectively with the wisdom of hindsight. Communicative contact would be realized only in cumbersome situations where extensive discussions indicate that there has been an *identity* of conceptions all along. We would then learn only by experience—at the end of a long process of wholy tentative and provisional exchange leading to actual agreement—that we were actually communicating. Communication would always require the wisdom of hindsight. And all our attempts in this direction would come to stand on very shaky ground. For no matter how far we push our inquiry into the issue of an identity of conceptions, the prospect can never be precluded of a divergency lying just around the corner—waiting to be discovered if only we pursued the matter just a bit further. One could never advance the issue of the identity of focus past the status of a more or less well-grounded provisional *assumption*. And then any so-called communication is no longer an exchange of information but a tissue of frail conjectures. The communicative enterprise would now become a vast inductive project—a complex exercise in conjectural theory-building, leading tentatively and provisionally towards something which, in fact, the imputational groundwork of our language enables us to presuppose from the very outset.[3]

How do we really know that Anaximander was talking about *our* sun? He is not here to tell us. And he did not leave elaborate discussion about his aims and purposes. How, then, can we be so confident of what he meant to talk about? The answer is straightforward. The key is the factor of *putative* intent—of an outright presumption or supposition on our part. That he is *to be taken* to talk about *our* sun is, in the final analysis, something that turns on two very general issues in

---

[3] The nature and the justification of such imputations is treated more fully in ch. 9 of the author's *Induction* (Oxford, 1980).

which Anaximander himself actually plays little if any role at all: (1) our subscription to certain generalized principles of interpretation with respect to the Greek language, and (2) the conventionalized policy of ours of ascribing certain fundamental communicative policies and intentions to other language-users in general. It is these predeterminations of ours that provide for communicative contact.[4] In the face of appropriate functional equivalences we allow neither a difference in language nor even a difference in 'thought-worlds' to block an identity of reference when this suits our purposes.

Our use of language is governed by a pivotal postulation of an *intention* to communicate about common and objectively self-subsisting objects—forgoing any and all claims to regard our own conceptions of these objects as being definitve or decisive. And this intention—the indispensable foundation of all communication—is not something personal and idiosyncratic. It is nowise a biographical aspect of certain particular minds but a shared feature of 'social mind', built into the custom-established ground rules of a social group's use of language as a publicly available communicative resource. The wider social perspective is crucial. In subscribing to the conventionalized intention at issue, we sink 'our own point of view' in the interests of entering into the wider community of fellow communicators. Only by admitting the potential distortion of one's own conceptions of things can one manage to reach across the gulf of divergent conceptions so as to get into communicative touch with one another.

The information that we ourselves may have about a thing, be it real or presumptive information, is always just that— information that *we* lay claim to. We cannot but recognize that it is person-relative and in general person-differentiated. Objectivity as such is something far more basic. For our attempts at communication and inquiry are undergirded by an information-transcending stance, the stance that we

---

[4] The point here is that the intention at issue need not be a biographical fact about a communicator. (After all, where no shared beliefs whatever are assumed, intentions are hard to infer from communicative behaviour.) The 'intention' at issue is *imputed to others from the outset* as a matter of general policy, rather than *learned or discovered ex post facto* from the substance of their declarations.

communally inhabit a shared world of objectively existing things—a world of 'real things' amongst which we live and into which we inquire but about which we have and must presume ourselves to have only imperfect information at any and every particular stage of the cognitive venture. This is not something we learn. The 'facts of experience' can never reveal it to us. It is something we postulate or presuppose *ab initio*. Its epistemic status is not that of an empirical discovery, but that of a presupposition underpinning a transcendental argument for the very possibility of communication or inquiry as we standardly conceive of them.

Objectivity is grounded in assumptions and not in informative discoveries. The commitment to *objectivity* is basic to our discourse with one another about a shared world of 'real things' to which none of us is in a position to claim privileged access. This commitment establishes a need to 'distance' ourselves from things—i.e. to recognize the prospect of a discrepancy between our (potentially idiosyncratic) conceptions of things and the true character of these things as they exist objectively in 'the real world'. The ever-present and ever-acknowledged contrast between 'the thing as we view it' and 'the thing as it is' is the mechanism by which this crucially important distancing is accomplished. We subordinate the former to a concern for the latter. In this context, such a pretention-humbling stance is the price we pay for keeping the channels of communication open.

We have an ongoing commitment to a manifold of objective *things* existing as such in the real world—things that are themselves impervious to conceptual and cognitive change on the part of those who consider and discuss them. This commitment is built into the very ground rules that govern our use of language and embody our determination to maintain the picture of a relatively stable world amidst the ever-changing panorama of cognitive world-pictures. The continuing succession of the different states of information are all linked to a pre- or sub-scientific view of an ongoing 'real world' in which we live and work, a world portrayed rather more stably in the *lingua franca* of everyday-life communication and populated by shared things whose stability amidst cognitive change is something rather *postulated* than learned.

This realistic world-projecting stance that the things that we encounter in experience are the *subjects* and not the *products* of our inquiries lies at the basis of communication. It undergirds and implements our determination to adopt a world-view that makes it possible to exchange information—to impart and extract information in a setting in which we communicate with one another about the issues that concern us.

If our talk about things pivoted on the precondition of having others share the same conception about them, the whole communicative project could never get under way. And this would lead straightaway to the unpleasant result of a cognitive solipsism that would preclude reference to inter-subjectively identifiable particulars, and would thus block the possibility of interpersonal communication. In sum, consensus—agreement of beliefs and conceptions—just is not a critical requisite for successful communication. (It is not a *sine qua non* but—at best—a useful aid to efficiency.)

8.4 *Communication Can Dispense with Shared Beliefs and Values*

One could, in theory, try to project a 'transcendental argument' from the centrality of consensus via the idea that it forms part of the 'conditions under which alone' a communicative community (or, for that matter, a viable social order) can be established:

Co-ordination/collaboration among people is a necessary condition for interpersonal communication (or: for a viable social order)

A consensus on interactive process is a (virtually) necessary condition for co-ordination/collaboration among inter-agents

---

Therefore: Consensus/agreement is a (virtually) necessary condition for interpersonal communication (or: for a viable society)

But this plausible-looking argument breaks down owing to the unavailability of its second premiss. It is simply false that consensus (that is, an agreement of beliefs) is a necessary condition to achieve co-ordination and collaboration among people in situations of human interaction.

What is crucial for your ability to communicate with me—to convey to me information about your beliefs, plans, or values—is not that we have a commonality of beliefs or ideas, and so stand in a consensus of some sort, but something quite different. It pivots on the recipient's capacity to *interpret*—to make good inferential sense of the meanings that the declarer is able to send. In the final analysis the matter is not one of an *agreement* between parties but of a *co-ordination* between them on the basis of a recipient's unilateral capacity effectively (successfully) to interpret the substantive resources of a source's declarations.

In his explication of the social aspects of communication, Karl-Otto Apel maintains that there are certain formal presuppositions for speech acts, certain claims that a speaker 'must' make when he enters into communicative interchange—such, for example, that he himself is sincere and that what he accepts is true.[5] A speaker's commitment to the idea of reaching a rational accommodation with his interlocutor lays the basis (as Apel sees it) for developing a 'transcendental argument' *via* a presuppositional regress to a logical basis for reaching a rationally constrained consensus on the basis of mutual commitments. But this is highly problematic. To establish communicative contacts, people must draw inferences from experiential givers—they must engage in inductive and hypothetical reasoning. But they need not do so in the same way. I can derive communicative benefit from your declarations without thinking about the issues in the same way you do. Otherwise experts could not communicate with lay people—or conversely. To enter into a dialogue or discussion does not *presuppose* a common commitment to shared principles, however much it may be facilitated thereby. In the final analysis, it is always up to the hearer (receiver) to construe a speaker's declarations—and to do so he need not necessarily enter the speaker's frame of mind or intentions.

---

[5] Karl-Otto Apel, 'Fallibilismus, Konsenztheorie der Wahrheit, und Letztbegründung', in W. R. Köhler *et al.* (eds.), *Philosophie und Begründung* (Frankfurt am Main, 1987), 116–211. See also his *Diskurs und Verantwortung* (Frankfurt am Main, 1988).

The crux for what people take away from communicative interactions is not what speakers purport but what their hearers credit them with. The issue does not hinge on a consensus or agreement between speaker and hearer, but on what the hearers are able to take away through inference—largely on the basis of suppositions and imputations that they themselves bring to the communicative context.

To derive communicative benefit we must, clearly, be able to *interpret* the other party's contribution. But doing this certainly does not require a commonality of beliefs and conceptions. Consensus on issues will doubtless *facilitate* efficient communication but it is certainly not a *requisite* for it. There is, in this regard, a crucial difference between what makes communication possible and what makes it easy. Consensus may help in this latter regard, but for the former it is dispensable. What counts is not *agreement* but simply the capacity to *interpret*. And interpretation is possible across a gulf of disagreement. (How else would we understand the scientific writings of the ancient Greeks, let alone their mythology and theology?) For there to be communication between two parties there must indeed be suitable sort of co-ordination between their thinking. But consensus—substantive agreement—is not part of what is required. It is not belief-coincidence but interpretative access that provides the linkage that underlies the information transmissions at issue.

Consensus of idea may make communication easier, but it is nothing fundamental. It is facilitative rather than essential. Communication does not require consensus—not agreement in beliefs, opinions, and ideas—but something quite different, namely a commitment or determination (prejudgement, postulation, presumption, supposition) on the part of a recipient interpreter to do whatever can reasonably be done to extract information from the declarations at issue. Here 'can reasonably be done' adverts to what is do-able within the range of procedures and policies that have met the 'test of experience' in past employment. For *efficient* communication (rather than for communication as such, pure and simple) consensus is unquestionably a help: the more we agree, the more readily we can get by with mere hints and clues. But it is a very far cry from this consideration to the (deeply problematic) idea that consensus is required for there to be effective communication at all. For at this level what is required is a certain degree of declarative talent on the part of senders and interpretative talent on the part of recipients.

What communication demands is accordingly (1) the determination to impart information to people and to extract information from their declarations, and (2) the prudent and judicious implementation of this determination by sensible means (i.e. by means which have a 'track record' of effectiveness). The salient fact is that our successful mutual communication about shared objects is *not* predicated on consensus—on an agreement in our conceptions of the items at issue—but rather roots in a resolve or determination 'to keep in touch', to do what is practicable to transmit information and to draw communicative benefit from the pronouncements of others. To re-emphasize: In the context of communication, it is the hermeneutic factor of *interpretation* (with all its many-sided ramifications) rather than the social factor of *agreement* that is paramount for establishing the cognitive contact necessary to the project.

But does communicative interchange not presuppose agreement on certain values: staying in touch, keeping the conversation going, working towards common understanding, trying to diminish the regions of disagreement, and the like? And does this not constitute a certain degree of procedural (albeit not necessarily substantive) consensus? Not necessarily.

Take 'keeping the conversation going'. Clearly if one party breaks off, there's an end to the exchange. But what continuity requires is surely a co-ordination of procedure, and not an agreement on any value. Each of the parties can continue to keep in touch with the others *for its own distinctive reasons*, which may go off in very different directions. I may keep in dialogue with you in order to secure information about what you think (which I don't accept at face value at all). You may keep the discussion going in order to convince your aunt Mabel of your goodwill towards me. The lesson is plain: communicative interaction involves a procedural co-ordination that can *but certainly need not* proceed from an agreement as to ends or from a consensus of values.

8.5 *Does Communication Presuppose a Pursuit of Consensus?*

With respect to matters of information and knowledge, people can in principle and do in practice agree or disagree at different values of consideration—at different depths, so to speak. Their agreements/disagreements can relate to:

1. *Theses* (claims, contentions): The answers that they give to the questions about the facts of the matter.
2. *Reasons*: The sorts of grounds that will count for or against theses: what counts as evidence.
3. *Standards*: The ways and means of weighing evidence and accessing the nature and extent of its bearing. (Contentions as to how level (2) bears on level (1).)
4. *Objectives*: The ultimate purposes by which the bearing of standards and reasons upon the evaluative issues are determined. It is, primarily, the quest for reliable information and for effective guidance for practice that delineates the cognitive interpose as such. (Considerations as to the ends and purposes for which level (1) considerations are instituted.)

Considerations at level (1) are substantive, at levels (2)–(4) methodological. Considerations at level (4) relate to ends, at levels (1)–(3) to means. What we have overall is a depth hierarchy of issues involved in the project of knowledge-acquisition, the cognitive enterprise, so to speak.

To what extent must rational beings agree about these matters? The most helpful construction of this issue is not to interpret it as a question of 'the nature of rational beings as such'. Rather, it is to interpret it in terms of our own stance towards what we would accept as rational—what we would expect of someone we were prepared to regard as such. And in this regard, the salient point is that if we are confronted with aberrant responses at a level that is sufficiently deep, then we are simply no longer minded to accept the agents involved as proceeding rationally. The ruling principle is this: The deeper the level at which dissonance and disagreement occurs, the less we are minded to see the agent as proceeding rationally: *the deeper the disagreement, the less we can regard it as* rational *disagreement.*

We can accept that someone who disagrees with us about 'the facts of the matter' may nevertheless still qualify as proceeding rationally (on the basis, for example, of different reasons, different evidence). But if there is disagreement even as to what sorts of things *count* as reasons, or—even worse— what the standards and critics that determine the bearing of one's reasons in one's class, then our inclination to see irrationality at work becomes almost irresistible. And finally, if our interagent does not even concur in our view as to the cognitive aims and objectives, then we simply cannot see ourselves as engaged in a process of rational interaction. Someone not involved in adhering to those principles and objectives is not engaged with us in a process of rational discussion (whatever else they may in fact be doing).

But what we have to do with here is *not* a discovery about the nature of rational beings, rather it is a regulative presumption or presupposition of our own about the nature of rational processes of informative interaction. That our inter-agents are rational in this regard is a regulative preconception on our part—something that we bring into the context of social interaction from the very first rather than something that we may take away from it at the end. (To be sure, the presumption at issue is a defeasible one which the course of events may lead us to abandon.)

In this light, the agreement we suppose to obtain with the interlocutors when we engage in rational discussion and cognitive interaction is no more than a regulative presupposition of the enterprise. It is not a factually discovered consensus but at most a retrospectively confirmed prejudgement. Thus 'consensus' is not a prerequisite for rational discussion, but merely a defeasible presumption made by those who enter into a communicative interaction of this sort.

From this point of view, it emerges as informatively placed to look at the issue from the agent's point of view. From the communicative agent's point of view, the object of the enterprise is not (necessarily) to reach *agreement* with his or her interlocutor on the issues under discussion. The primary objects of communication are (1) to *extend* one's information and (2) to *solidify* one's information (by testing it against the facts and opinions available to others and seeing if any reasons to change one's mind come to view). And in this regard even disagreement is informatively useful—after all, it suggests that we may not 'have it right' after all. Reaching an *agreement*—the aligning of one's views with those of one's interlocutor—is almost certainly not a substantial part of the communicative agent's objective. The alignment of views—the reaching of a consensus on the issues—is neither a precondition nor a goal of the cognitive enterprise.

To be sure, when we communicate with others we generally do give them a certain credit. And, in particular, if we invest our time and effort in carrying on a rational discussion with them, then we generally acknowledge their cognitive competence, presumably being prepared at least to entertain the idea that they 'may have it right' after all. But this is something very different from either (1) hoping—let alone expecting— that they will align their views with ours, or (2) being prepared to move in the direction of conforming our views to theirs. To repeat and re-emphasize: the inherent aim of rational discussion is the enlarging and/or substantiation of our own information—it is not a matter of reaching agreement with others.

Jürgen Habermas's theory of communicative action holds that (rational) speakers presuppose that the achievement of consensus is the ultimate goal of communication: that agreement among communicators is the implicit aim of the communicative enterprise.[6] As Habermas sees it, rational people enter into situations of communicative interaction on the basis of a presumption that agreement can be reached. But this plausible-sounding supposition takes an overly ambitious line. The expectations of realistic people are not pitched quite so high. When they enter into communicative interaction with others, they proceed on the basis of the presumption that even

---

[6] See e.g. the essay on 'Social Action and Rationality' in Habermas, *Jürgen Habermas on Society and Politics*, ed. S. Seidman (Boston, 1989), 142–69. Habermas continues the two premisses that 'Reaching understanding (*Verständigung*) is the inherent telos of human speech' and that 'Reaching understanding is a process of reaching agreement (*Einigung*) with any speaking and acting subjects' (pp. 157–8). He thus co-ordinates speech (*logos*) with the pursuit of agreement. The idea of an exchange of information with others to clarify and define our differences in order to come to terms with them in a practical manner moves outside the orbit of Habermasian conceptions.

though agreement will (in all probability) *not* be reached, various benefits will be realized. In communication, it is not agreement but intelligibility that is the name of the game; what we both hope for and expect is not *endorsement* but *information*. What experienced and realistic communicators expect to achieve in communicative exchange is 'a mutual clarification of positions'—an understanding of where the other party stands and *why* this involves commitments that differ from ours (in so far as it does so). Only in the most ideally favourable circumstance would we expect a communicative interchange to issue in actual agreement—in consensus. Rational people are not utopians; they do not expect that their fondest and furthest hopes will be realized. They will be quite content to come away from a communicative situation with a result that goes no further than an improvement in their own understanding.

But, so Habermas insists, even to enter into discussion is to accept certain ground rules of communicative intention, and this involves a procedural consensus of sorts. However, the matter of what sort of 'consensus' is to be at issue is rather hard to formulate. Who or what is to say that one of us has not conceived to mislead, deceive, subvert? To be sure, each of us enters into a convention with certain *assumptions*—but these may or may not turn out to be warranted. In communicative interactions as in other human interactions there are no unconditional promises—and no guarantees. The idea that successful communication presupposes a substantive consensus is deeply mistaken.

But is it not the implicit objective of all (rationally conducted) communication to reach an agreement among the communicating parties with respect to the subjects at issue? If I tell you that something is so, is it not my aim and purpose to have you accept this and consequently agree with me, thus bringing our views on the issue into alignment? Well—that very much depends. I may be trying to deceive you. Or I might simply be 'testing the waters' to explore the extent of our agreement. Or—firmly expecting that you won't believe me—I might be discharging a responsibility to let you know what I believe. The possibilities are literally endless. Perhaps in certain sorts of communicative situations the reaching of agreement in a 'meeting of minds' is the ruling ideal. But it is certainly far from being the case that in most actual communicative situations the parties involved set out with the presupposition that reaching consensus is the object of the enterprise. (We seldom proceed on the supposition that our ideals are going to be realized in the real world.) As long as we provide for the possibility of using each others' declarations as a basis for plausible conjecture, consensus of conception and belief is not required. It is the imparting of our respective thoughts and ideas and not their co-ordination and uni-formization that is, surely, the paramount task of communication.

To be sure, as Habermas sees it, the pursuit of rational consensus is not only a normative or regulative *ideal* of rational discussion but is also its salient constitutive *presupposition*; it constitutes the inherent *telos* that defined the enterprise. If the discussants did not join in a common commitment to a shared view on the basis of mutually acknowledged reasons, then— whatever else they might be doing—they would not (as Habermas sees it) be involved in a rational discussion, a pointful communicative interchange. But this view surely requires a substantial qualification. For while rational discuss-ants do perhaps enter into their communicative exchanges with a view to the *possibility* of reaching a meeting of minds, they certainly need not have an *expectation* that this will actually happen. The fact is that in so far as consensus-seeking is a presupposition of rational discourse, this is so only in the *ideal* rather than the *real* order. The praxis of communication as it actually exists has a very different aspect.

9

Is Consensus Required for a Benign Social Order?

9.1 *The Question of Practical Consensus*

It is instructive to examine some of the more or less 'political' aspects of consensuality in the context of decision-making in the public forum. In particular, it is worthwhile to consider the demand for a *practical* consensus about what is to be done in the setting of a social group, focusing on the question: 'Is consensus-seeking to be regarded as a prime imperative of rational social policy?'

In and of itself, consensus is clearly no absolute. The crucial issue is not that of the existence of a consensus, but of how it came to be formed: was this a matter of cognitively irrelevant processes like coercion, propaganda, brainwashing, and the like, or was it a matter of rational persuasion and victory in a Darwinian struggle in the free and open conflict of ideas? One has to worry about what it is that people are consenting about and why it is they are doing so. (Think of the precedent of Nazi Germany.) All the same, the idea has been astir in some European intellectual circles for many years now that a just and democratic society can be achieved only on the basis of a shared social commitment to the pursuit of communal consensus. Such a view insists that the public harmony required for the smooth functioning of a benign social order must be rooted in an agreement on fundamentals. Progress towards a congenial and enlightened society accordingly requires an unfolding course of evolving consensus about the public agenda—a substantial agreement regarding the practical question of what is to be done.

This general line of thought traces back to Hegel, who

envisioned an inexorable tendency towards a condition of things where all thinking people will share a common acceptance of the manifold of truths revealed by Reason. Sailing in Hegel's wake, Karl Marx looked to the disappearance of social diversity in the triumph of a communist order in which people's clashing ideas and discordant social interests ('class conflicts') give way to the undisturbed uniformity of a shared communist polity and materialist philosophy. To this historical convergence, Friedrich Engels added an emphasis on the uniformizing impetus of modern science in defining a region where the ideas of all reasonable people must come together. More recently, the influential writings of Jürgen Habermas have done much to foster the view that a benign public order must be grounded in a commitment to the ideal of consensus. To be sure, Habermas substitutes for the actual historically evolving consensus of Hegel and his followers the Peircean idea of an asymptotic approach to a *focus imaginarius*— an idealization that historical reality will only approximate but never reach. Nevertheless the insistence on uniformity and co-ordination (*Gleichschaltung*) remains. In the tradition of German social thought that reaches from Hegel through Marx to the Frankfurt School and beyond, the idea has emerged with increasing prominence that the realization of a communally benign social order requires a commitment to consensus— a shared public commitment to the idea that the pursuit of consensus in communal affairs is a great and good thing.

This position, however, is deeply problematic. A good case can be made out for the contrary view that a benign social order need not be committed to the quest for consensus, but can be constituted along very different, irreducibly *pluralistic* lines. After all, the idea that a consensus on fundamentals is realistically available is in fact false with respect to most large, complex, advanced societies and is (so we shall argue) simply not needed for the benign and 'democratic' management of communal affairs. And even the idea that consensus is a desirable ideal is very questionable.

To be sure, the widely favoured allocation of a pride of place to consensus sounds benevolent, irenic, and socially delectable. Indeed, it may sound so plausible at first hearing that it is difficult to see how a person of reasonableness and goodwill could fail to go along. Nevertheless, there is room for real doubt as to whether this utopian-sounding position makes sense. Serious questions can be raised as to whether the best interests of a healthy community are served by a commitment to consensus.

To begin at the end, let it be foreshadowed that the policy whose appropriateness will be defended here is one of a *restrained dissonance* based on an acceptance of a diversity and dissensus of opinion—a benevolent (or at any rate resigned) acceptance of the disagreement of others with respect to beliefs and values. Such an approach envisions a posture of diversity conjoined with 'live-and-let-live', taking the line that a healthy democratic social order can not only tolerate, but even—within limits—welcome dissensus (disagreement, discord), provided that the conflicts involved are kept within 'reasonable bounds'. The present discussion will accordingly maintain the merits of the consensus-dispensing view that a benign social order can be unabashedly pluralistic, and based not on the pursuit of agreement, but on arrangements that provide for an *acquiescence in disagreement*. This position sees as perfectly acceptable a situation that is not one of homogeneity and uniformity, but one of a dissonance and diversity that is restrained to a point well short of outright conflict and chaos.

Not only is insistence on the pursuit of general consensus in practical matters and public affairs unrealistic, it is also counter-productive. For it deprives us of the productive stimulus of competition and the incentive of rivalry. In many situations of human life, people are induced to make their best effort in inquiry or creative activity through rivalry rather than emulation, through differentiation rather than conformity, through a concern to impede the folly they see all around. Productivity, creativity, and the striving for excellence are—as often as not—the offspring of diversity and conflict. Dissensus has this to be said for it, at least, that it is at odds with a stifling orthodoxy. A dissent accommodating society is *ipso facto* pluralistic, with all the advantages that accrue in situations where no one school of thought is able to push the others aside.[1]

---

[1] For an eloquent advocacy of the benefits of social pluralism see John Kekes's stimulating book, *The Morality of Pluralism* (Princeton, NJ, 1993).

Far from its being a consensual homogeneity of belief and value that is the mark of a benign social order, a good case can be made out that it is a mutually accommodating diversity that is pivotal. The extent to which a society exhibits tolerance—is willing and able to manage with an aconsensual diversity arising from free thought and expression—could be seen as a plausible standard of merit, since a spirit of mutual acceptance and accommodation is one of the hallmarks of a benign and productive social order.

9.2 *Some Examples of Productive Modes of Dissensus*

Crucial for these deliberations is the distinction between productive or constructive modes of disagreement and dissensus on the one side, and on the other those modes of discord that are unproductive and destructive. To bring this distinction into clearer view, it is useful to contemplate some concrete examples of decidedly positive social arrangements that are based on accepting dissensus rather than pursuing consensus.

Few-Party Electoral Systems. Electoral systems of the few-party, winner-take-all type familiar in the English-speaking democracies involve an adversarial process that is very remote from any sort of consensus-tropism. In such systems, issues are resolved by majority vote (or some close cousin thereof), rather than by mechanisms that militate towards the formation of a communal consensus of the sort at issue (for example) in the business meetings of the Quaker sect. Political decisions are transacted through an open conflict between rival parties competing for adoption by the electorate or their representatives of the particular policies, programmes, and people that these parties favour. The process takes the form of an open struggle for the support of a mere majority (of voters, parliamentary representatives, etc.), rather than attempting to bring everyone into the range of a communal consensus. Such a procedure is fundamentally adversarial rather than consensual. What counts in the final analysis for the effectiveness of this recourse to voting as an approach to public decision-making is not that by its means everyone (or almost everyone) is won over to an agreement as to the rightness of what is being done, but rather that people are prepared to receive the decisions arrived at with peaceful acquiescence, even when they may be convinced that these decisions are wrong.

Anglo-American Legal Procedures. In the Anglo-American tradition, legal proceedings, be they civil or criminal, are strictly adversarial procedures. The system does not endeavour to bring the conflicting parties into the consensus of a voluntary or constrained agreement: its very heart and soul is conflict and adversarial antagonism. Once a case actually comes to trial, its resolution is not reached by negotiation, compromise, and consensus-formation among the parties involved, but rather imposed on the conflicting parties from without—i.e. by 'the judicial system'.[2] Again, what ultimately matters is not that the parties accept the appropriateness of the resultant resolution ('reach a consensus'), but is simply that they yield—that they acquiesce, however reluctantly, in the resolution that 'the system' imposes upon them.[3]

Binding Arbitration. Binding arbitration is now widely used in developed societies as a process for settling conflicts in labour relations and for resolving contractual disputes. In such situations, the arbitrator is not, however, a 'marriage counsellor'—a negotiation facilitator who tries to bring the parties to a consensual meeting of minds, leading them towards a commonly aggreable solution that they will mutually regard as just and proper. On the contrary, so far as those two conflicting parties are concerned, the process is a fundamentally adversarial one. In the end, the arbitrator will generally determine a solution which the parties themselves will most likely regard as thoroughly imperfect and undesirable, but in which, presumably, they will reluctantly acquiese

[2] To be sure, there are exceptions here. Within the jury deliberation process, the law requires actual (or virtual) consensus, and 'plea bargaining' does call for a negotiated agreement. But these consensual islands stand in a sea of competitive adversary processes.

[3] Ideally, to be sure, this acquiescence will reflect a general acceptance of procedures as being just even when particular outcomes are deemed incorrect. But realistically, even the procedures are often deemed faulty, and their resolutions nevertheless accepted with disgruntled resignation because the alternative to acceptance is deemed impracticable.

because carrying the dispute further would, in the circumstances, involve a balance of costs and benefits that compares unfavourably with the balance secured by acquiescence.

Intellectual Conflicts. Throughout science, scholarship, and the professions, there is a pervasive conflict among rival ideologies, methodologies, or theories. In virtually every setting of intellectual endeavour (any profession, discipline, or speciality), the phenomenon of rival 'schools of thought' is commonplace. Such schools of thought are in a condition of conflict and rivalry, competing for the adherence of 'the larger community' and—perhaps most importantly—for that of posterity. The work of scientific and academic specialities in particular will, by and large, proceed not by a communally co-operative search for consensus, but rather through an—often productive—rivalry between conflicting schools of thought, each with a variant position of its own, and all competing for attention and allegiance within the wider group. Competition and the divergence of commitments that it carries in its wake is pervasive throughout these domains.

As such examples show, there are various reasonable, productive, and thoroughly 'democratic' social processes that are based not on an actual or desired consensus, but on the pluralistic acceptance of dissensus—not, to be sure, for its own, inherently positive sake, but because of a recognition that this flexibility effectively serves the interests of the general benefit. It is, after all, central to the characteristic genius of the Anglo-American system of parliamentary government and legal process that these institutions are founded not on a pursuit of consensus but on essentially adversarial procedures.

9.3 *Productive Versus Unproductive Modes of Conflict*

It must be acknowledged straightaway that dissensus does have a negative side. Its negativities pre-eminently include:

1. The danger of escalation from productive competition to destructive conflict.
2. The possible diversion of resources (effort and energy) into potentially unproductive forms of rivalry.

3. The Balkanizing fragmentation of the community into groups estranged from each other in a posture of mutual hostility.

4. The tendency to dismiss otherwise meritorious plans, projects, and ideas simply because they originate from the 'outside', from a rival, competing source.

Clearly, the story is not straightforwardly one-sided. However, the sensible way of handling the question of consensus vs. dissensus calls for effecting an appropriate balance between the positive and the negative aspects of the issue, seeking the productive advantages of tolerating dissent while averting its potential negativities by *ad hoc* mechanisms fitted to the specific circumstances at hand.

This said, the fact remains that it is highly problematic to maintain that a rational public policy must be predicated on a striving for consensus. Situations where the public good is best served by a general acquiescence in disagreement are not only perfectly possible but often actual. Life being what it is, it would be too hard on all of us to be in a position where we had to reach agreement in matters of opinion and evaluation. A society in which the various schools of thought and opinion try to win the others over by rational suasion is certainly superior to one in which they seek to do so by force or intimidation. But this does not automatically make it superior to one where these groups let one another alone to flourish or founder in their divergent individuality. After all, the striving towards consensus produces a sometimes debilitating uniformity of thought, and the tolerance of diversity permits the flourishing of an often fruitful diversity of individual plans, projects, and visions. Pluralism on the other hand can often better serve the currently prevailing interest of individuals, securing for them and for their society the potential future benefits accruing from a stimulating competition and productive rivalry.

The course of social wisdom regarding consensus accordingly lies not in its all-out pursuit, but rather in a judiciously limited acceptance of dissensus. The pivotal consideration is to secure the benefits of rivalry and competition while circumscribing its negative and potentially harmful aspects within manageable bounds. This is certainly not a matter of fostering dissensus for its own sake—which would indeed be foolish—but rather one of accepting and even welcoming it in so far as this can be productive of good in the larger social scheme of things.

9.4 Acquiescence and Controlled Conflict

Consensus by its very nature is a condition of intellectual uniformity, a homogeneity of thought and opinion. And just herein lie some of its significant shortcomings. For the fact is that the impulsion to consensus will in various circumstances prove itself to be:

1. An impediment to creativity and innovation. (Settling into a consensus position is a discouragement from endeavouring to outdo others and striving to improve on their efforts by 'doing one's utmost to excel'.)
2. An invitation to mediocrity. (By its very nature, realization of consensus involves a compromise among potentially divergent tendencies and thus tends to occupy 'the middle ground' where people are most easily brought together, but where, for that very reason, the element of creative, insightful innovation is likely to be missing.)
3. A disincentive to productive effort. (One of the most powerful motives for improving the level of one's performance is, after all, to come under the pressure of competition and the threat of being outdone by a rival.)

Most human intellectual, cultural, and social progress has begun with an assault by dissident spirits against a comfortably established consensus. The Andalusian friar Bartolomeo de las Casas upheld the human rights of Amerindians against the consensus of Spanish conquistadores and settlers alike that they were inferior beings; the eighteenth-century American abolitionists protested the institution of slavery in the teeth of a vast preponderance of powerful opponents; J. S. Mill's protest against 'the subjection of women' was a lone voice crying out in a wilderness of vociferous males. And lest it be said that such 'eccentric' but benevolent views did all eventually win through to a general consensus of thought and universality of practice, one can instance the teachings of Jesus whose consensual endorsement by Christians is largely a matter of words and not deeds. We can have no comfortable assurance about the present—or future—consensual victory of truth, justice, and the cause of righteousness.

When we find ourselves dissenting from others, we may dislike their opinions and disapprove of their actions—and they ours—but we can, by and large, manage to come to terms. The fact is that in our mutually satisfactory dealings with other people—whether in matters of belief or of action—we need not proceed on the basis of consensus and agreement. We can—often, at least—'get along' with others quite adequately when we can 'agree to disagree' with them or when we can simply ignore, dismiss, and sideline our disagreements—postponing further opposition to another day. What matters for social harmony is not that we agree with one another, but that each of us acquiesces in what the other is doing, that we 'live and let live', so that we avoid letting our differences become a *casus belli* between us. ACQUIESCENCE is the key. And this is not a matter of *approbation*, but rather one of a mutual restraint which, even when disapproving and disagreeing, is willing (no doubt reluctantly) to 'let things be', because the alternative—actual conflict or warfare—will lead to a situation that is still worse. All is well as long as we can manage to keep our differences beneath the threshold of outright conflict.

A good illustration is afforded by a historical episode. Shortly after the end of the Civil War, in early 1866, Robert E. Lee, generalissimo of the just-defeated Confederacy, was asked to testify before a hostile Joint Committee on Reconstruction of the US Congress. Interrogated about the stance of the former secessionists towards Washington's plans and programmes for them, Lee was pressed on whether the Southerners agreed with these and whether (as Senator Jacob M. Howard put it) 'they are friendly towards the government of the United States'? Choosing his words carefully, Lee replied, 'I believe they entirely *acquiesce* in the government'.[4]

---

[4] Marshall W. Fishwick, *Lee After the War* (Westport, Conn., 1963), 112.

The difference between *acquiescence* and *agreement* cannot be shown much more clearly.

An insistence on the primacy of communal consensus is something too idealized, too unrealistic, too academic. The ultimate result of discussion, debate, and controversy is generally not to develop the homogeneity of agreement and consensus, and to demand this would be a totally unrealistic aim in a pervasively diversified world. The sensible object is to avert discord—to keep the temperature of conflict low in matters of belief and action, and where possible to limit discord and disagreement to the verbal arena. The advantage of rational discussion is not that it ultimately leads to agreement, but that—even in the face of sharp disagreement—it generally serves to keep down the temperature of conflict, seeing that as long as we talk we do not fight. Recognizing the difficult realities of this world, the sensible community of interagents is not involved in discussion in an idealized quest for agreement; it is involved in discussion because as long as we discuss matters with one another, we avert other, more painful forms of conflict.

Philosophical contractarians see justice to consist in the instituting of arrangements that are (or would be) reached through reasoned interchange among the affected parties in idealized conditions (being unconstrained, equal in power, etc.).[5] All the same, if this is what 'justice' is, then 'life is unjust' (as J. F. Kennedy observed). In real life we confront not an institutional *tabula rasa* but a historically given reality, and we have to do not with people as abstract interchangeable units, but with flesh-and-blood individuals affected by the realities of capacities, talents, and empowerments. Real-life social arrangements must, in the end, turn not on what people would have if they ideally could, but on what people are prepared to do and to accept. Real-life politics is the art of the possible.

But what of those cases where a society must decide, and where even inaction constitutes an action of some sort—such cases as abortion, or the death penalty, or gun control? In

---

[5] See e.g. David Gauthier, 'Constituting Democracy', *Lindley Lecture Series: University of Kansas* (Kansas City, 1989), 7.

such situations, the need for a communally established resolution faces us with the unpleasant alternative of either consensus or the subordination of the interests of some to those of others. And here it needs to be emphasized that in seeking for social accommodation, consensus and domination are not the only alternatives. The choice is not just between the agreement of the whole group or the lordship of some particular subgroup. Accommodation through general acquiescence is a perfectly practicable mode for making decisions in the public order and resolving its conflicts. And, given the realities of the situation in a complex and diversified society, it has significant theoretical and practical advantages over its more radical alternatives.

The crucial fact about *acquiescence* is that it is generally rooted not in *agreement* with others but rather in a preparedness to get on without it. What makes good practical and theoretical sense is the step of (on occasion) accepting something without agreeing with it—of 'going along' despite disagreement—an acquiescence of diversity grounded in a resigned toleration of the discordant views of others. The merit of such tolerance is not (as with John Stuart Mill) that it is an interim requisite for progress towards an ultimate collective realization of the truth, but simply and less ambitiously that it is a requisite for the peace and quiet that we all require for the effective pursuit of our own varied visions and projects.

A deep strain of utopianism runs through social-contract theory, be it of the Rawlsian form favoured among North American social philosophers or the Habermasian form in vogue on the European continent. Historical experience, empirical understanding of the human realities, and theoretical analysis of our social situation, all conjoin to indicate that an insistence on agreement among rational inquirers and problem-solving agents is simply futile. However inconvenient for the philosophers, ample experience shows that not only in matters of politics, art, and religion, but also in a whole host of cognitive domains like history, economics, social science, and philosophy, we shall never actually achieve a firmly secured general consensus. And there is no reason to think that a benign society can exist only where the clash of private opinions and preferences is eliminated or suppressed by the processes of social co-ordination. A healthy social order can perfectly well be based not on agreement but on the sort of mutual restraint in which subgroups simply go their own way in the face of dissensus.

Neither in intellectual nor in social contexts, after all, have we any firm assurance that a consensual position somehow represents the objectively correct or operationally optimal solution. To be sure, in many cases some sort of resolution must be arrived at with respect to public issues. But we need not *agree* about it: a perfectly viable result may be had simply on the basis of a grudging acceptance of diversity. What matters for the smooth functioning of a social order is not that the individuals or groups that represent conflicting positions should think alike, but simply that they acquiesce in certain shared ways of conducting society's affairs.[6]

A viable society can dispense with consensus (the USA is a pretty good example). What it cannot dispense with is a fair degree of acquiescence—as the recent history of the Lebanon or of Yugoslavia amply illustrates.

It is instructive to recognize that acquiescence is not really the same as *compromise*. Like compromise, acquiescence involves acceptance of an alternative which the parties involved see as suboptimal. But compromise involves (1) some sort of explicit effort at reaching a mutual accommodation,

---

[6] Gauthier, in a perceptive passage, contrasts those who are *friends*—who co-operate out of ties of mutual concern—with those who are *opportunists* in seeing one another as a useful means to the furtherance of their own ends. He contemplates: 'The interaction of those who would prefer not to interact, each of whom regards the presence of the others as a cost, may, in the most favourable circumstances, result in a *modus vivendi*. Now it may be that, having acquiesced in such a situation, the participants come over time to regard it differently, to realize that the others afford opportunities as well as imposing costs. The others are, if not yet welcome, nevertheless useful, their presence accepted and not merely and grudgingly tolerated. Persons who were once enemies, now find themselves allies. . . . Their only bonds are those of convenience. . . . Opportunities for mutual benefit are seen to arise only in limited areas of life, and to be restricted to activities that are valued merely instrumentally . . . [and] bonds between persons may remain ones of mere convenience' (ibid. 4). Neither Gauthier nor I view this sort of situation, of negativism turned to self-interested co-operation, as the most advantageous and desirable of imaginable relationships. But nevertheless, a society which cannot promote, maintain, and utilize a great deal of it will not—people being what they are—be able to realize a generally acceptable quality of life for its members.

whereas acquiescence can be quite passive, and (2) compromise generally involves seeking out and adopting the best available mutually acceptable arrangement, whereas the parties involved may well acquiesce in something inferior though still tolerable. For example, let two parties have the preference-ordering schedules as between four alternatives (*A–D*) as shown in Table 9.1. Assuming that both see *B* and *C* as 'something they can live with', an effort to *compromise* would probably lead the parties to *B*. But if *C* is already fixed in place and has the saliency of an accomplished fact, then the parties may nevertheless acquiesce in it—and quite sensibly so if costs or uncertainties are involved in a shift to *B*.

In a well-ordered pluralistic society, each dissensual party will only try 'up to a certain point' to convince the others of the rightness of its position. Beyond this point, it will simply resign itself to the acceptance of disagreement, dissonance, and diversity on a 'live-and-let-live' basis. The sensible—and realistic—polity of a viable public order is not consensus through agreement, but a pluralistically fertile disagreement mitigated by acquiescence through a recognition that the conflicts at issue are acceptable and that the price to be paid for conflict resolution is unacceptably large because the means through which such agreement would be established are too costly, seeing that they would involve an escalation from discussion to force, from controversy to conflict. The stability and tranquility needed for the constructive management of a society's business need not root in agreement—and not even in a second-order agreement in the processes for solving first-order conflicts—as long as the mechanisms in place are ones that people are prepared (for however variant and discordant reasons) to allow to operate in the resolution of communal problems.

TABLE 9.1.

(1)	(2)
A	D
B	B
C	C
D	A

Acquiescence, of course, can cover a fairly wide span across the spectrum ranging from willing to reluctant. (But it has its limits. The bank manager who opens the safe because his family is being held hostage is not acquiescing—he is simply being coerced.) All the same, the fact remains that no workable social or political system can be based solely and entirely on willing agreement alone, forgoing any and all reliance on acquiescence that is reluctant. In so far as acquiescence provides an effective instrument of conflict resolution it will—in the difficult circumstances of real-world affairs—frequently have to be obtained reluctantly. Of course, on the other side of the coin, there is also the fact that no system will be viable in the long term if the acquiescence it elicits is too often and too deeply reluctant.

From this point of view, it is a prime social desideratum to realize a framework of interaction that renders dissensus harmless, inducing people reciprocally to acquiesce in opinions and actions with which they are in fundamental disagreement, because of the favourable overall balance of benefits over negativities that acquiescence engenders (among other things through the fact that in granting the privilege of nonconformity to others, people generally protect it for themselves).

9.5 A Consideration of Some Objections

In an interesting recent discussion, John Rawls has elaborated the idea of an 'overlapping consensus' among subgroups with diverse beliefs, goals, interests, and ideologies, as a vehicle for agreement on fundamentals in a pluralistic society.[7] Rawls sees this as a means of resolving the difficult issue of reconciling 'social rivalry in a democracy' with the absence of 'a shared conception of the meaning, value, and purpose of human life'.[8] Accepting pluralism at the substantive level of

---

[7] John Rawls, 'The Idea of an Overlapping Consensus', *Oxford Journal of Legal Studies*, 7 (1987), 1–25. Rawls initially introduced the notion in his *A Theory of Justice* (Cambridge, Mass., 1971), 388.   [8] Rawls, 'Idea', 1–2.

ideologies and values, Rawls looks in particular to a *consensus on the issue of procedural justice* to make possible the effective transaction of public affairs in the face of real disagreement: 'The point of the idea of an overlapping consensus . . . is to show how, despite a diversity of doctrines, convergence on a political conception of justice may be achieved and social unity sustained'.[9] Now of course no sensible person will deny the conditional thesis that *if* there is consensus on procedural matters (be it based on a common commitment to justice or some other basic methodological value—fairness, rationality, or whatever), *then* social unity can obtain in the face of pluralistic diversity because of the overriding force of this common instrumentality of difference-adjudication. The critical question is not *can* social unity in a congenial pluralistic society be based on a procedural/methodological consensus, but *need* it be so based? Do we need a higher level consensus to sustain the organic viability of an internally diversified society? Must a viable public order rest on a consensus—if not on substantive then at least on procedural matters?

We come, at this juncture to what is a central point in the defence of our present position. It pivots on the following objection put forward by a hypothetical critic:

> I agree with much of what you have said on the merits of dissensus and diversity. But you have failed to reckon with the crucial distinction between a consensus on matters of ground level *substance* and a consensus on matters of *procedure*. As you maintain, a benign social order can indeed dispense with a substantive consensus regarding *what* is decided upon. But what it indispensably requires is a procedural agreement on modes of conflict resolution—a second-order consensus about *how* those first-order issues are to be decided. If the social order is to serve effectively the interests of those involved, and if mutual strife and conflict are to be averted, there must be a consensus on *process*, or the validity of the procedural ways in which these base-level resolutions are arrived at. Consensus on particular

[9] Rawls, 'Idea', 5.

decisions may be dispensable, but consensus on the decision-making *process* is essential.

Despite its surface plausibility, even this more sophisticated argument for the necessity of an at least procedural consensuality is deeply problematic.

For one thing, even where there is a consensus about process, there may nevertheless be sharp disagreement regarding matters of implementation. Even where people agree on, say maintenance of law and order, civility of interaction, an equitable distribution of resources—and many other such 'procedural' principles of human action in the public domain—such procedural agreements are much too abstract to define particular public policies. (We can agree on the need for 'law and order' and yet (quite plausibly) disagree sharply on questions of civil disobedience and the limits of appropriate protest.) Process consensus is a lot to ask for—but still is not sufficient for a benign social order.

But the problem goes deeper yet. For it is also false that procedural agreement is necessary for a benign social order. To manage its affairs in a mutually acceptable way, a community requires no agreement on the merits of those procedures as long as there is acquiescence in their operation. What matters is *not* that we agree on methods—I may have my favourite and you yours. (I might, for example, think that the proper way to address the issue at hand is for the electorate to decide it by referendum; you think that the right and proper way is by a vote in the legislature.) But as long as we both acquiesce in the established process of having the courts decide, all is well. There is no *agreement* here: we emphatically do not concur in thinking that the courts are the proper (let alone the best!) avenue for a solution—in fact, *neither* of us thinks so. What we do is simply acquiesce in what the courts make their decisions on the issue. What matters for irenic conflict resolution is not second-order consensus but second-order acquiescence. A sensible defence of acquiescence is accordingly not predicated on ignoring the distinction between first-order substantive issues and second-order methodological ones: rather it is prepared to turn this distinction to its own purposes and to see it as advantageous rather than inimical to establishing the claims of acquiescence *vis-à-vis* consensus.

Again, consider the objection:

> Surely consensus is the controlling factor. After all, does not acquiescence itself represent a consensus of sorts? Do those conflicting parties who acquiesce on a given solution not in fact agree in accepting this?

The response here is to grant that acquiescence is indeed a *co-ordination* of sorts—it puts the parties into an alignment. But it does not involve their *agreeing* to anything. To 'go along' with a resolution and to 'live with' it is not to *agree* in something; it is simply to refrain from upsetting the applecart. Acquiescence and 'going along' is not tantamount to consensus.

But even when we 'agree to disagree' do we not in fact agree? Not really. Or, rather, we do so in name only! An agreement to disagree is as much an agreement as a paper dragon is a dragon—the whole point is that there is no agreement at all here. Parties who agree to disagree do not *agree* on anything—they simply exhibit a similarity of behaviour in that they walk away from a disagreement. They no more agree than do bouncing billiard balls that move away from one another.

Another possible objection to an emphasis on acquiescence as a mechanism of social decision runs as follows:

> To cast acquiescence in a leading role in the management of public affairs is to invite the deployment of raw power; to open the doors to coercion, oppression, domination, and the subjection of the weak to control by the strong.

But this view of the matter is simply unjust. The rational person's acquiescence is, after all, based on a cost–benefit calculation that weighs the costs of opposition against the costs of 'going along'. And to deploy raw power is to raise the stakes—to readjust not only the benefits but also the costs of acquiescence. As those who study revolutions soon learn, it is precisely at the point when power is made blatantly overt— when bayonets are mounted and blood shed in the streets— that acquiescence is most gravely endangered. It is clear that discernibly just, benign, and generally advantageous arrangements will secure the acquiescence of people far more readily and more extensively than those that infringe upon such obvious social desiderata. It is quite false that an approach that roots social legitimacy in acquiescence somehow favours oppression and injustice.

To be sure, much will depend on the sorts of people one is dealing with. If they are unreasonably longsuffering and spineless—if they are weak-kneed and cave in easily under pressure—then a social order based on acquiescence is one in which they indeed can be oppressed and exploited. (But then, of course, if they are totally accommodating and yielding, a consensual order based on agreement with others is also one in which their true interests are likely to suffer.) The fact remains that sensible people are distinctly unlikely to acquiesce in arrangements that are oppressive to them. An acquiescence-oriented political process does not provide a rationale for domination, exploitation, and oppression precisely because these are factors in which sensible people are unlikely to acquiesce—once brought into play they soon call forth opposition rather than accommodation. One of the early lessons that an acquiescence-based society learns is that its ways are not smoothly viable if people are constantly testing the limits of acquiescence. An emphasis on being civilized, urbane, and restrained is not at odds with a reliance on acquiescence but the reverse is the case, the achievement of acquiescence is easier whenever these virtues prevail.

It is instructive also to consider another objection that moves in a rather different direction from the preceding:

> To cast acquiescence in a leading role in the management of public affairs is to invite non-co-operation and recalcitrance. For the unscrupulous can withold their acquiescence and try to force people to meet their terms. Acquiescence-seeking accordingly favours the wilful, stubborn, cantankerous.

Apart from its holding equally well for consensus tropism, this objection overlooks the fact that recalcitrance is not cost-free. People who block social accommodation by holding out stubbornly against generally acceptable compromises lose friends, undermine trust, destroy sympathy—and thereby undercut their prospects of prevailing if not presently then on future occasions.

Consensus and acquiescence are alike in this respect, that in the real world they both represent factual rather than normative arrangements, so that—in consequence—something more must be added if the issue of legitimacy is to be addressed. With consensus, we want to ensure that it is freely given, adequately informed, and sensibly motivated agreement that is at issue. And with acquiescence essentially the same factors will be operative. The qualifications needed to effect an appropriate transition from the factual to the normative level will be substantially identical on both sides, and the comparative advantages of the two factors must, in the end, turn on other considerations.

The important thing, in any case, is that the complaint that a polity of acquiescence inherently favours the perpetration of injustices cannot be sustained. Acquiescence is like agreement in this, that nobody else can do it for you. People may be able to rearrange the conditions under which you will have to proceed in this regard, but how you proceed within those conditions is always in the final analysis up to you. As recent developments in Eastern Europe all too clearly show, people will only acquiesce in injustice up to a certain point. After that they turn to non-co-operation and opposition—they take up arms against the sea of troubles or perhaps simply emigrate. The limits of acquiescence are finite.

There will, of course, be situations in which it makes good sense to strive for consensus. Sometimes the benefit of having others 'on board'—of averting a situation of disaffection and dissatisfaction on the part of people—will outweigh the cost of further effort, expenditure, and time required by efforts to convert them. (This is particularly true when one is dealing with basically reasonable people who are caught up in a basically unreasonable position.) But much of the time this is not the case because these conditions for plausible consensus-formation are simply not met. (In the USA, you simply are *never* going to work the National Rifle Association's membership around to accepting hand-gun control by rational suasion; this social desideratum can be obtained only through creating circumstances in which they acquiesce, no doubt unwillingly, in an arrangement they do not like.)

Admittedly, acquiescence can be bad—it can be forced or compelled. It is no automatic route to political legitimacy. But then of course neither is consensus. We are always entitled to ask why people agree: is it for good and valid reasons—a concern for truth or for fairness, say—or is it because of self-interest, conformism, constraint, or propagandism? Legitimacy is always an additional issue: and even as it is not just consensus one wants but a consensus that is rational and free, so it is not just acquiescence one wants but acquiescence that is given in a way that is given reasonably.

9.6 *The Rationale of an Acquiescence-Oriented Approach*

The question of the rationale for acquiescing in dissensus deserves closer examination. Viewed from a decision-theoretic perspective, the decisive point is simply that the evaluation of consensus-seeking calls for a complex balancing of benefits against costs. For consider the following state of affairs regarding my own alternatives for proceeding in a situation of disagreement between us:

Benefits
1. I secure your agreement to my position: B_A
2. We continue to differ: B_D

Costs
1. I expend the further effort needed to secure your agreement: C_A
2. I accept your continuance in a discordant position: C_D

The deciding factor for the rational resolution of a dissensus-tolerance decision is clearly that of an overall cost–benefit relationship among the values/disvalues at issue:

$$B_A - C_A > ? < B_D - C_D$$

Letting $G_X = B_X - C_X =$ the net gain of a given (X-indicated) position, the question comes down to the straightforward comparison:

$$G_A > ? < G_D$$

That is: Does the net gain of working for agreement outweigh the net gain of accepting a dissensus? And there is no reason of abstract general principle for thinking that, in many or most social-interaction situations, the ultimate resolution of such a cost–benefit assessment must inevitably and automatically favour the cause of agreement and consensus.

The point is simply, and crucially, that two factors must be balanced off against each other:

1. The cost of effective opposition to a given measure or arrangement in the interests of moving the group to an agreement on an alternative that one deems preferable.
2. The cost of going along with the measure one deems unsatisfactory.

Thus, consider the situation of a disagreement between two parties ('You' and 'I') neither of which is minded simply to yield to the other. Each of us faces the choice between (1) interfering with the other in order to impel them towards thinking or doing what suits our own desires, or (2) letting the other be with each of us going our own way. There will thus be four possible situations; as at Table 9.2. From my point of view, (b) is the most pleasing prospect, and (c) the worst; for you the inverse situation obtains. And if our respective capacity to cause difficulties for the other party is (as we may suppose) more or less equal, then (d) is preferable to (a) for each of us. Thus my preference ranking is (b), (d), (a), (c). And your preference ranking will correspondingly be (c), (d), (a), (b). The interaction situation is thus as depicted in Table 9.3 which combines our respective preference-schedules into the unified picture of a hypothetical 'game'. The resultant interaction situation exemplifies what has become known as a

TABLE 9.2.

	I	You
(a)	interfere	interfere
(b)	interfere	let be
(c)	let be	interfere
(d)	let be	let be

'Prisoner's Dilemma'.[10] For each party, the first choice is dominant: in opting for one's first alternative each will automatically fare better irrespective of the choices made by the other. On standard game-theoretic principles, mutual interference therefore emerges as the indicated conclusion, and 3/3 emerges as the favoured result.

But this outcome is clearly bizarre, seeing that each of us would in fact prefer to achieve 2/2 and would, undoubtedly, reach this compromised result in a negotiation conducted as equals. Something has gone amiss when the issue is regarded in its standard game-theoretic maximum perspective to issue in a recommendation of mutual interference. A different analysis is required—and available.

The crux lies in that the overall situation here is clearly one that is (by hypothesis) altogether *symmetric* for the two parties proceeding rationally on the basis of the given information. Given this situational symmetry, whatever rational consideration will constitute a possible motive for the one party consequently also does so for the other: everything that makes sense for the one makes sense for the other, thanks to the 'mirror-image' relationship. The outcome of a rational choice will thus have to lie on the diagonal—these being the only 'circumstantially available' symmetrical solutions. The rationally realistic choice is accordingly that between the two diagonal-located positions of mutual interference and mutual letting be. And here the latter is clearly preferable to *each* party.

Resignation to an 'agreement to disagree' is clearly the sensible solution here. And we reach this sensible resolution

TABLE 9.3.

	You interfere	You let be
I interfere	3/3	1/4
I let be	4/1	2/2

[10] Regarding this problem and its literature see Richmond Campbell and Lanning Snowden, *Paradoxes of Rationality and Co-operation: Prisoner's Dilemma and Newcomb's Problem* (Vancouver, 1985).

because people come to acquiesce in the diversity of others since the available alternatives are worse. To be sure, neither of us then gets what we ideally want—namely, that the others yield to us. But we are situationally constrained to settle for second best in order to avert a still less desirable outcome. In such circumstances, acquiescence in diversity and dissensus is the best policy, being motivated not by a coincidence of goals, but by a perception of common benefit. And while the situation of our schematic example is not universal, the fact remains that this general sort of situation is frequent enough to invalidate the claims of consensus-seeking as a social imperative.

Even if we could agree on what ideally rational people would do under ideally rational circumstances, this would provide precious little guidance as to how to proceed in the real world. Knowing how to play a perfect hand in a card game will not help us to decide how to play the imperfect hands that fate actually deals to us. Knowing how to proceed in ideal circumstances gives little or no guidance as to how to proceed in sub-ideal conditions. A theory geared to utopian assumptions can provide little guidance for real-life conditions. What is needed is, clearly, a process attuned to the suboptimal arrangements of an imperfect reality. And at this stage a validation based on the principles of 'rational decision theory' has much to be said for it.

As these deliberations indicate, a perfectly sensible approach to the rational legitimation of the political process can substitute for the contractual-idealization approach of social-contract theory (Rawls), or ideal-consensus theory of 'discourse ethics' (Habermas and Apel), the older and better-known mechanism of rational decision—the good old cost–benefit rationality of orthodox decision theory.[11] And against the 'utopian unrealism' of the contractarian and consensus

---

[11] In several places (e.g. ch. 7 of *Rationality* (Oxford, 1988) or ch. 4 of *Risk* (Lanham, Md., 1983)), I have criticized rational decision theory on grounds of comprehensiveness and completeness, maintaining that there are various sorts of special situations where rational decision theory does not apply, or perhaps even leads us amiss. However, such a denial of any imperialistic claims to all-sufficiency and all-pervasive authority does not invalidate the claims of the approach to provide a useful mechanism for handling the bulk of cases in the prosaic range of ordinary, unproblematic situations, the present context included.

theorists, the present approach takes the more 'realistic' line of hard-nosed cost–benefit economics.[12]

The salient point is that acquiescence in a situation of (duly limited) conflict and competition can—and often does—have something to be said in its favour, in principle as in practice. Agreeing neither in opinions nor in ends (goals, objectives, values), people can nevertheless be led to go along with the disapproval or diversity of others through a realistic realization that, in the circumstances, the cost of working to redirect their thinking into the paths of agreement is simply too high. In many cases, seeking to transmute disagreement with outright conflict would be to divert resources unproductively from a satisfactory pursuit of our own projects.

9.7 Is Consensus a Requisite for Co-operation?

There yet remains, however, the further large and complicated question: Is consensus not in fact a *precondition* of co-operation? If this were indeed so, then the case on behalf of consensus would be secure. For it is clear that without co-operation among the people in a society a satisfactory life cannot be achieved.

However, the matter in fact stands otherwise. In innumerable situations in life it is desirable—even necessary—for two parties to co-operate with one another. But for such co-operation to occur there need be no *consensus*—no actual agreement, be it on ends or on means. You vote for candidate X because you think he will improve the postal system (which is a desideratum of yours). I vote for him because he is my brother-in-law and I like the idea of having a relation in high office. So you vote for X, and I (who am not a registered voter of the district) dissuade Y from voting against him. We co-operate in effecting X's election, but neither the means (voting for him; dissuading someone from voting against him), nor the ends (providing a better postal system, placing a relative in high office) are the same in our two cases.

Admittedly, agreement can facilitate co-operation in various

---

[12] To be sure, it leaves open the larger, deeply problematic issue of whether these costs and benefits are to be *seeming* ones or *genuine* ones.

sorts of circumstances. (Though it can also engender rivalry—
as when two young men both agree that a certain girl is the
most desirable match in town.) But agreement is not an
indispensable requirement for co-operation. Indeed, outright
disagreement will frequently engender co-operation—as when
two rival candidates for a given office, each of whom deems it
best that he himself should hold it, co-operate in frustrating a
third.

The key consideration for the conduct of interpersonal
affairs is that the activities of people can harmonize without
their ideas about ends and means being in agreement. It is a
highly important and positive aspect of social life that people
can and do co-operate with one another from the most diverse
of motives; agreement need not enter into it at all. What is
needed for co-operation is not consensus but something quite
different—a *convergence of interests*. And it is a fortunate fact of
communal life that people's interests can coincide without any
significant degree of agreement between them (a circumstance
illustrated in both domestic and international politics by the
frequency with which allies fall out once the war is over).

Like traditional socialist theoreticians, Habermas insists on
having an abstractly universal and collective basis of agreement; a convergence based on concrete, particular commonalities of interest and value is not good enough for him. But
realism and generosity alike compel us to realize that co-
operation among real people is based on the concrete realities
of their personal situation—and to exploit this fact as best we
can in the best interests of the community at large.

Habermas and Apel both resort to the Kant-reminiscent
tactic of grounding the political legitimacy and normative
validity of a benign social order in the methodological
presuppositions of rational public discourse—as facets of the
'condition under which alone' productive communication can
transpire in the public forum. This proceeding encounters two
difficulties:

  1. Those methodological presuppositions of rational public
     discourse are profoundly *underdeterminative*—they are too
     abstract and contentless to yield any concrete results.
     (In these matters process without substance is perhaps
     not blind but certainly too near-sighted.)

2. The theory mirrors the overly optimistic Greek idea that if only we would reason aright we would automatically act for the best—that right reason could and would abolish the diversity of self-interest.

In consequence the idea that 'discourse ethics' suffices to underwrite political legitimacy is fundamentally unrealistic and unrealistically utopian.

To be sure, this charge is resisted. In an interesting essay on the question 'Is the Ethics of the Ideal Communication Community a Utopia?'[13] Karl-Otto Apel endeavours to rebut such a line of criticism. Acknowledging that consensualism is 'utopian in the negative sense of extreme irrelevance' to our real-life, practical activities, Apel sees this utopianism as harmless. After all, considerations of political realism do not, as such, touch the issue of the validity of our ethical ideals. However, this sort of response misses the point, which is that issues of ethical idealization ('what we would ideally like, considerations of realism aside') is totally distinct from the question of political legitimacy ('what is to be seen as acceptable and appropriate as a way of persuading in the circumstances that confront us?'). We cannot frame our educational policies on the basis of what ideally intelligent, diligent, and co-operative students would do. No more can we frame our political arrangements on the basis of how a community of ideally rational, informed, and impartial citizens would conduct their affairs.

A political process that is both theoretically valid and practically workable must seek not to *abolish* divisive self-interest but to *co-ordinate* it. It must provide for a system of interaction within the orbit of which co-operation of individuals for the greatest common good ('the best interests of the community as a whole') becomes an integral component of the interests of each. And this requires not methodology alone (and certainly not just the methodology of deliberative reasoning), but substantive mechanisms of co-ordination, that is, the forging of a community of consilient interests.

It is clear that a social polity geared to acquiescence rather

---

[13] Tr. in S. Benhabib and F. Dallmayer (eds.), *The Communicative Ethic Controversy* (Cambridge, Mass., 1990), 23–59.

than consensus-formation will call for a rather different sort of social engineering approach. The one calls for all the instruments of rational suasion, salesmanship, and propaganda needed to align people in the same way of thinking. The other calls for forgoing conditions under which people can recognize and exploit a confluence of interests in spite of their different ideas and objectives, thus being led into the ways of co-operation by shareable benefits rather than by common ideas. What matters is not *shared goals* but the recognition of a common interest in conflict management.

A consensus-geared polity is perfectly well and good where it can be had. But the harsh realities of a fragmented world make it eminently desirable—indeed imperative—to have a way of achieving co-operation among those who simply are not likeminded. A polity based on acquiescence has the substantial advantage that it can secure collaboration and co-operation even where the individuals at issue fail (as is all too common) to accord with one another in respect of their beliefs, desires, goals, and values. It puts the rationale of social polity on a more workable and realistic basis in a difficult, sub-ideal world.

What is needed for social harmony is not consensual disagreement-removal (i.e. insularity and parochialism) but a mechanism for the limitation of conflicts. And it is surely mistaken to think of the latter (consensus) as the best—let alone the only—means to the former (conflict management). Consensuality will be a paramount social value only when one has to do with people to whom one cannot credit a reasonable amount of good sense. For only for the narrow-mindedly intolerant will disagreement issue in conflict and diversity of opinion in social friction.

If consensus were the only or best viable instrument of conflict management, then consensuality would indeed become a prime social desideratum. But surely this is (or should be) far from being the case in a sensible society. A benign social order can and must be able to exist and thrive despite diversity. It need not be predicated on agreement, but can exist on the basis of restraint and forbearance, a willingness to live and let live and to respect the due rights and claims of others irrespective of whether we agree with them or not. Friendly personal *companionship* may indeed require a significant sharing of opinions and values, but a reciprocally beneficial social *community* requires no more than a shared context and a convergence of interests.

Actual *agreement* among the interacting parties—however convenient and desirable—is thus nowise necessary for co-ordinating people's actions and activities in a way requisite for the realization of interpersonally fruitful arrangements and the forging of social harmony. For a co-ordination based on mutual forbearance and reciprocal acquiescence is sufficient. And this is all to the good, seeing that the realities of human nature and society are such that actual agreement in such matters cannot realistically be expected. After all, there are interests and interests. When people's basic interests and projects differ and they are at odds with each other in the pursuit of clashing objectives, then it is—all too often—pointless to push for a consensus, a 'meeting of minds'. But this circumstance need not be as ominous as it may seem on first view. For the most promising course in social engineering is not a generally foredoomed quest for consensus, but the creation (if need be *ex nihilo*) of a set of operating ground rules of social interaction that engenders a situation in which the 'on second thoughts' interests of people lie in the direction of mutual accommodation. (Exactly this, after all, is the prime function of a system of 'law and order'.)

In terms of philosophical anthropology, it would seem that insistence on consensus simply gets it wrong. At the most fundamental level, what links the human community together is not agreement but understanding. It is not that we do or will agree with one another—there is simply too much interpersonal variability for that. Rather, it is that every person can potentially and in principle interrelate with every other and enter into some relationship of sympathy, empathy, and comprehending fellowship.[14] It is for excellent reason that the saying goes *tout comprendre c'est tout pardonner* and not *tout accepter*.

The impetus to consensus has its strongest roots not in

<hr>

[14] This is manifested by the virtually universal appeal of a well-wrought good biography of practically anybody.

substantive but in psychological considerations. The widespread appeal of consensus-seeking is perhaps best explained in terms of a human need for group solidarity—for inclusion in a community and acceptance by one's social group. *Homo sapiens* is a social being: our need for social acceptance is comparable to our need for physical and mental nourishment. Finding ourselves in a condition of agreement with others is unquestionably a source of comfort. But given the ultimate unavailability of a pervasive consensus, it is a merciful fact that, be it in a family or larger group, social solidarity and co-operation need not be based on actual agreement, but can be rooted in a mere convergence of interests.

In sum, then, there is good reason to reject the idea that consensus is a prime desideratum of rational social policy. A cogent case can be made out for holding that the prime social imperative is not towards consensus but towards something very different—the forging of a system of interaction that makes possible a peaceful and even substantially co-operative coexistence with others in the face of unresolved and perhaps even unresolvable disagreement. A polity that accepts pluralism and diversity while at the same time broadening the domain of shared interests and fostering arrangements that encourage people to acquiesce in the differences of others has much to be said in its favour.

But what of the moral impetus? In cases where I take myself to see the right way, do I not have consensus-promoting duty to induce or encourage others to change their views accordingly? Do I not have an obligation to 'set them straight'? Well, for one thing, in some cases it may be in my best interests— that is for *my* advantage—to bring them around to my view of the matter. But this sort of thing is clearly a matter of self-advantage and not of duty. On the other hand, it may be a matter of their best interests—that is, of *their advantage*—to be put right. But then the question becomes a quantitative-comparative one of balancing off (among other things) *how much* it is in their advantage against *how much* it is to their benefit to be left alone—not to have someone else intrude upon them. For, clearly, in this context as in others there is a big difference between helpfulness and meddling. In any event, the controlling factor here is not consensuality as such but simply the moral consideration of due attention to the best interests of people.

But is not a situation in which people agree clearly better than one in which they simply go along—is consensus not inherently preferable to acquiescence when other things are equal? Yes, of course it is. With 'other things equal' or 'in ideal conditions' agreement is certainly better than disagreement and consensually achieved resolutions preferable to those achieved through reluctant acquiescence. But philosophers who maintain this sort of position subject to such saving qualifications seldom admit how precious little follows from it. Other things are seldom if ever equal and conditions seldom if ever ideal. In this world, we live and labour among complex sub-ideal circumstances, where matters seem very different once we look beneath the *prima-facie* surface and recognize that different things are seldom if ever equal. What matters first and foremost is not the design of a utopia but the devising of mechanisms for coping with the problems of the real world. And in dealing with these actual problems a recourse to idealizations can be both unprofitable and counter-productive. What is wanted here is not utopianism, but the design of institutions that can move real-world, imperfect, crassly motivated individuals into courses of action that serve the general benefit. And at *this* level, a recourse to programmes and policies based on acquiescence has much to be said for it.

If we wish to have a sensible and relevant account of political legitimacy then we have to construe the issues not in terms of what people would agree on in idealized (but in fact unrealizable) conditions, but in terms of what is viable in the real world. And then, it is not hypothetical consensus but practicable acquiescence that becomes the pivot-point.

Such deliberations highlight the flaw of a social philosophy which, like that of Jürgen Habermas, puts the pursuit of consensus so high on the scale of the socio-epistemological values that it becomes—quite inappropriately—a *sine qua non* for social rationality as such. Consensus, to re-emphasize, can be and often is no more than an agreement in folly.

Problems of Consensus as a Political Ideal

10.1 *A Political Perspective*

The ancient Sophists viewed consensus as the bearer of special powers. As they saw it, individual people have their idiosyncratic opinions and desires—each person goes his own way and is a law unto himself (*homo mensura*: 'man is the measure of all things', as Protagoras taught). Nature itself determines no norms: no right or wrong, good or bad. But what nature (*phusis*) leaves undetermined, human consensus can supply through custom (*nomos*). The ground rules of a viable public order are instituted by a society in which convention distils certain *common* interests out of the *individual* interests of each separate member—for example, the common interest in 'law and order'. Consensus lies at the basis of a viable political order. The centrality of consensus has thus been on the agenda of Western political philosophy from the very outset.

A great continental divide runs across the philosophical landscape. On the one side lies the Platonic tradition that looks to systemic order through a rational co-ordination under the aegis of universal principles. On the other the Aristotelian tradition that looks to organic balance and an equilibration of diversity and division. The one is geared to a classicism of holistic order, the other to a pluralism of countervailing checks and balances. The one favours the rational uniformity of a harmonious consensus, the other the creative diversity of a limited dissensus. The one invokes the tidiness of theorizing reason, the other the diversified complexity of natural and social history.

Given this divide, European political thought since the time of the Enlightenment has been fixated upon the idea of the 'general consent' of the people in defining a general agreement of the community (*la volonté générale*) which may or may not be all that apparent to the people themselves (and may need to be discerned on their behalf by some particularly insightful élite). All the same, the dangers of that idea, run amok, is apparent to anyone who has looked, even casually, into the history of the French Revolution.

The polity of consensus proceeds from a fundamentally socialistic commitment to the co-ordination and alignment of individual action into the uniform social order of 'rationalized' central planning (albeit, no doubt, a uniformization that is not imposed, but rather engendered—presumably—through the 'hidden hand' of an idealized rationality). By contrast, the polity of pluralism abandons the goal of a monolithically unified 'rational order' for the 'creative diversity' of a situation of variegated rivalry and competition. Its political paradigm is not that of a command economy with its ideal of rationalization and uniformizing co-ordination, but that of a free market with its competitive rivalry of conflicting interests. Consensuality looks to uniformity of thought, pluralism to reciprocally fruitful harmonization of discordant elements.

Jürgen Habermas laments the current situation in a philosophy and the social sciences as engendering a 'new incomprehensibility'—a situation of disagreement and diversity, manageable only by means of a 'peculiar syncretism' (*einen eigentümlichen Synkretismus*).[1] It is clear that such a 'chaotic' situation of confusing diversity and plurality offends Habermas's sense of rational tidiness. After all, the mainstream tradition of Western social and political philosophy exhibits a strong penchant for homogenity and uniformity. Consensus—agreement in thought—is demanded as essential to a 'social contract' among collaborating equals mutually pledged to strive for positions on which all are equally agreed. To a broad spectrum of political and social theorists the idea that a viable 'social order' can actually be in substantial degree *disordered* in

---

[1] Jürgen Habermas, *Die neue Unübersichtlichkeit* (Frankfurt am Main, 1985); see pp. 132–7.

being based on dissensus and pluralistic diversity seems anathema. Isaiah Berlin has observed this clearly:

No one today is surprised by the assumption that variety is, in general, preferable to uniformity . . . Yet this has not long been so; for the notion that One is good, Many—diversity—is bad, since the truth is one, and only error is multiple is far older. . . . Who in the ancient world or in the middle ages ever spoke of the values of diversity in life and thought? But when a modern thinker like Auguste Comte wondered why, when we do not allow freedom of opinion in mathematics we should allow it in morals and politics, his very question shocked J. S. Mill and other liberals. Yet most of these [diversity-tolerant] beliefs are relatively novel, and draw their plausibility from a deep and radical revolt against the cultural tradition of western thought.[2]

Legislatures, taxing authorities, and political theorists all like to keep the affairs of the citizenry neat and tidy. But the fact of the matter is that the impetus to public consensus, agreement, and concurrence of thought will not be high on the priority list of the true friends of personal freedom and liberty.

As Habermas sees it, what is good for people, what human flourishing is all about, is what the members of a community come to agree on its being when they operate in conditions of unfettered deliberation and discussion—free from distortion and coercion.[3] Properly founded social consensus is the definitive arbiter of the human good.

But of course here there is the all too realistic prospect that even a rational society of unconstrained deliberators may (nay almost certainly will) find it impossible to arrive at a consensus view of the human good because different individuals will take different views of the matter. One would clearly be well advised to provide for a view of human flourishing that is based on dissensus. The virtually inevitable fact that different groups take different and discordant views of the matter throws a big monkey wrench into Habermas's theory of a social good that is available only through consensus and co-ordination.

---

[2] Isaiah Berlin, 'The Apotheosis of the Romantic Will', in *The Crooked Timber of Humanity* (London, 1990), 207–37; 207–8.

[3] Jürgen Habermas, 'Wahrheitstheorien', as repr. in G. Skirbekk, *Wahrheitstheorien* (Frankfurt am Main, 1977).

What an insistence on the social primacy of consensus overlooks is that while in a healthy social order people must *get along* with one another, they need not for this reason *go along* with one another in what they think. People of radically different ideas can co-operate without agreement and coexist without consensus.

Rather different sorts of policy approaches are at work in social orders based on consensus-oriented and acquiescence-oriented principles. Consensus-seeking societies will aim to *maximize* the number of people who approve of what is being done; acquiescence-seeking societies seek to *minimize* the number of people who disapprove very strongly of what is being done. The two processes sound similar but are in actual fact quite different in spirit and in mode of operation. The one seeks actual agreement, the other seeks to avoid a disagreement so sharp as to preclude acquiescence.

The social requisite of a viable public order can thus plausibly be viewed as lying not in the fostering of consensus, but in the forging of conditions in which people become willing and able to acquiesce in dissensus through recognizing this as a state of affairs that is not only tolerable but even in some way beneficial. Consensus simply is not a requisite for the prime social desideratum of having people lead lives that are at once personally satisfying and socially constructive.

On this perspective, one arrives at a less tidy, less idealized, but nevertheless truer and more realistic picture of our social condition, one that accepts without regret the dissensus of a restrained rivalry among discordant and incompatible positions none of which is able to prevail over the rest. The upshot is one of reciprocal acquiescence in a pluralistic community of conflicting views—a situation in which each party is content to accept a diversity that affords them the benefit of pursuing their own projects at the cost of according a like privilege to others.

The relationship between consensus and the public good is thus complex: one cannot validly make simple generalizations about it. But nevertheless, the idea that the pursuit of consensus is essential to a rationally managed society on the grounds of its being a requisite for productive coexistence and social co-operation cannot withstand close critical scrutiny.

10.2 Problems of Idealization and the Search for a Realistic Middle Way

Habermas projects the idea of a discussion in the quest for consensus managed under ideal conditions (an 'ideal speech situation') in which the parties concerned proceed with

1. No constraint: every discussant is fully free to speak his or her mind.
2. Equal opportunity: everyone gets a fair and equal opportunity to contribute.
3. Equal power: no one is in a position to 'throw more weight around' than the rest—to impose pressure of some sort.
4. Rational processes: everyone seeks to persuade the rest by good reasons, rather than by threats, appeals to emotion or capacity, etc.

On this basis, Habermas maintains his positions (1) that the defining conditions of such an 'ideal speech situation' are identical with the conditions of an ideal political process (i.e. one that characterizes the political system that sensible people would ideally want to belong to is one that would arrive at its decisions by a consensus established by such a process), and (2) that for this reason, a consensus reached in such circumstances has a politically privileged position, and thereby provides a touchstone of political legitimacy.[4] For Habermas, accommodation and compromise are thus a poor second best to which the quest for consensus should never be subordinated.[5]

The shortcomings of this idealization-approach are two. (1) On the side of *method*, it prescinds too much from the realities

---

[4] For a particularly clear exposition of Habermas's position see his *Vorstudien und Ergänzugnen zur Theorie de kommunikativen Handelns* (Frankfurt am Main, 1984), 159–82. A clear, cogent, and thoroughly sympathetic exposition of Habermas's position is given in Thomas McCarthy, *The Critical Theory of Jürgen Habermas* (Cambridge, Mass., 1981); see ch. 4, 'Foundations: A Theory of Communication', for the range of considerations presently at issue.

[5] See his *Moral Consciousness and Communicative Action* (Cambridge, Mass., 1990). The unrealistic aspects of Habermas's position are sufficiently blatant that even his expositors and defenders are constrained to take notice of them. See e.g. Thomas McCarthy, *Ideals and Illusions: On Reconstruction and Deconstruction in Contemporary Critical Theory* (Cambridge, Mass., 1991), 197–9.

of the world—it is too idealized and utopian. And (2) on the side of *substance* we have the difficulty that the gap between idealized consensus and real-world problems is so large that the theory founders on problems of implementation. There is much justice in Albrecht Wellmer's claim that 'The idea of a social order that rests upon a procedurally unconstrained consensus of all its members is certainly not "empty"; however nothing directly follows regarding the *legitimacy* of its particular social institutions.'[6] The fact is that political legitimacy never follows from abstract process alone without considerations of substance. (After all, Adolf Hitler initially gained power through a democratic election.) Politics being 'the art of the possible', appropriateness in this context is always a comparative issue—a matter of determining the best of the *available* alternatives, with availability hinging crucially on the concrete realities of the given situation.[7] And to say that where all the available alternatives are so bad that we had better go back and find others is simply 'cheating',—since where other options can be found (or created) that initial list of alternatives was simply not complete—contrary to hypothesis.

In particular, it is instructive to consider the impetus to consensus in the light of a contrast between social pragmatism and social idealism. The social idealist position is characterized by its recourse to idealization in addressing matters of validation and legitimation. It has two basic versions:

Ideal Social Contact Theorists (e.g. John Rawls): A social arrangement is seen as valid (appropriate) to the extent that a society's members would—if perfectly rational—opt for it in ideal circumstances (the members being equally 'powerful', not acting under pressure or duress, equipped with all relevant information, etc.). On this approach, validation turns on considering an arrangement's place in a social contract achieved under ideal conditions.

Ideal Process Theorists (e.g. Jürgen Habermas): A social arrangement is seen as valid (appropriate) to the extent that it

---

[6] Quoted in S. Benhabib and F. Dallmayer (eds.), *The Communicative Ethic Controversy* (Cambridge, Mass., 1990), 325.

[7] This line of criticism is also pressed by Benhabib, ibid. 343.

is arrived at by a society's members through the processes and procedures that would govern an ideal discussion—i.e. a quest for consensus among perfectly rational agents acting in ideal circumstances (all equally 'powerful', not acting under pressure, equipped with the relevant information, etc.). On this approach, validation is a matter of the ideal appropriateness of the process by which an arrangement is arrived at.

There is, of course, a sharp contrast between such idealization theories of political legitimation and a

Pragmatic Optimization Theory: A social arrangement is valid (appropriate) to the extent that—comparatively among all the actually (realistically) available possibilities—it causes the least dismay: i.e. minimizes the overall extent to which people are seriously dissatisfied by its adoption. This approach of an inverted utilitarianism, as it were, assesses acceptability in terms of discontent-minimization, with both the extent and the depth of dissatisfaction with the alternatives taken into account.[8]

The crux of the pragmatic theory is to see it as concerned, not exclusively but extensively, to minimize the number of people that a given change in social *modus operandi* drives into a position of despair, and outright opposition. It strives not for the unattainable ideal of unanimous agreement, but for a high degree of acquiescence in which people are not necessarily eager but at least willing to go along with the measures at issue. As a theoretical position it enjoys, at any rate, the merit advantage of realism; in comparison to its idealistic alternatives it has the advantage of being true-to-life. The insistence of political theorists in the nineteenth century and beyond on idealized utopian models as a guide to praxis is profoundly illusory. Meaningful progress is made in this domain by improving upon what one has and not by trying to erect some

---

[8] Classical utilitarianism is now inverted, seeing that this pragmatic optimization is not a matter of 'the greatest good of the greatest number' but one of 'the least harm of the least number'. (Only if not harming were the sole form of operative benefit would the two approaches coincide.) Thus consider a distribution of benefits to three individuals, and compare $+2, +2, -1$ with $+1, +1, +1$. The first gives the greater good to the greater number, but the second reduces those actually harmed from 1 to 0.

idealized structure built upon its ruins. The history of modern Europe illustrates time and again the disastrous consequences for the well-being of ordinary people that flow from the well-meaning idealizations of a misguided utopianism. No doubt, the millenarians among us would yearn for a society organized on the principle of having people do what ideally rational agents would do in idealized conditions. But most of us recognize that this is simply pie in the sky. The pragmatic theory is clearly more realistic than its idealized rivals, seeing that it requires no recourse to perfectly rational agents and ideal circumstances. It is willing and able to function in 'the real world', pivoting its operation on a factor (the minimization of serious dissatisfaction and discontent) that is readily understood and relatively simple to assess.

The sensible posture, then, is to be realistic in the face of pluralism—to accept the unavailability of consensus, and to work at creating a communal framework of thought and action where we can come to terms with disagreement and make the best—and most—of it. Such a position calls for a profound change of methodological attitude to a distinctively different sort of social-engineering objective. The guiding principle is no longer 'Let us do whatever we can to promote consensus', but rather, 'Let us do whatever we can to render dissensus harmless—and even, wherever possible, profitable.' It is simply—and mercifully—wrong that consensus is the requisite for a stable society and a healthy body politic. It is simply—and mercifully—wrong that pluralism is the manifestation of an inherently harmful social malfunction.

After all, the idea that all should think alike does not augur all that well from a political standpoint. It was this emphasis on homogeneous thinking that brought us episodes like the expulsion of the Moors and Jews from Spain, the night of St Bartholomew in France, and analogous tragedies throughout recent history. No one can doubt that European civilization has paid and has exacted an enormous price for its canonization of consensus.

One's valuing coherence and rational uniformity in one's own thinking need not constrain a negative stance towards communal diversity. Dissensus and variety of opinion and valuation provides for enhancement rather than impoverishment of intellectual culture. A society that can come to terms with diversity—can manage to co-opt it into a peaceable and mutually stimulating interaction—is not made poorer by such a lack of consensus but is enriched by it.

Even if one grants (as one surely need not) that it is preferable, other things being equal, that people should agree rather than disagree, there remains the fact that in the real world other things are rarely altogether equal. And agreement, however desirable, is nowise *necessary* for the public good. The important and imperative thing is not to strive for consensus, but to try to create conditions of interaction where people can flourish despite (and perhaps even to some extent because of) a lack of consensus.

To accept diversity, to rest satisfied with dissonance, to live with the idea that others think differently from ourselves—even in this very matter of whether striving for consensus is a good thing—calls for adopting a certain sort of value scheme. It calls for rejecting both conformism (with its insistence that I should think like them) and chauvinism (with its insistence that they must think like me). It replaces both sorts of orthodoxy by a stress on urbanity, civility, and forbearance— by the spirit of live-and-let-live that is not so much a matter of 'tolerance' as of a respect for their autonomy and its correlative entitlement to do things in their own way.

A political or social order whose smooth operation requires consensus is simply too brittle and fragile for effective operation in this imperfect world. People are too varied of background, disposition, and experience to align their views of important public and social matters in a uniform consilience. Only a system that can function smoothly despite dissensus is theoretically adequate and practically viable. A satisfactory social system must function in such a way as to be acquiescence-engendering—that is, must be of a sort that people can clearly realize that by and large less is to be lost by acquiescence than by carrying matters further to try to constrain further agreement, be it through force, through propaganda, or through rational suasion. Life is simply too short for endless ventures in thought co-ordination. Precisely because the real-life decision problems in the political and social policy agenda require resolution in real time—then and there—it makes little sense to insist on an unachievable consensus, and is more realistic and practicable to accept whatever solution is minimally indefeasible in the circumstances, implementing it in such ways that the acquiescence of the discontented can be relied upon to do its pacificatory work.

10.3 *Is Consensus a Valid Ideal?*

Rational consensus on matters of belief and action is one of those absolutes that are seldom if ever at our actual disposal. No language, no belief system, no thought framework is absolute—delivered in unchangeable perfection to mankind by the world spirit from on high. In this life, we can do no more and no better than to make the best use we can of the limited, particularized, diversified opportunities that come to hand. And this general situation regarding the unattainability of *cognitive* consensus holds for evaluative and pragmatic consensus as well. All this of course, goes no further than to indicate that consensus is not actually *feasible*—that consensuality is an unrealistic demand. But of course the question remains, is it not nevertheless something eminently *desirable?*

No doubt, consensus is a desideratum of sorts—something it would be nice to have if we could get it under the right conditions, something to be welcomed where it can be found. But is it something whose pursuit we should insist on and persist in? Is it an appropriate ideal? There is good reason to think it is not.

To begin with, one must distinguish between an *ideal* and an *idealization*. An ideal as such belongs to the practical order. It is something that can and perhaps should be a guide to our actual proceedings, providing a positive goal—or at least a positive *direction*—of appropriate human endeavour. It represents a state of things whose realization—even if only in part—is to be evaluated positively and which should, by its very nature, be seen as desirable. Like 'liberty, equality, and fraternity', an ideal represents a state of affairs whose pursuit in practice is to be regarded as pre-eminently 'a good thing'. By its very nature as such, an ideal is something towards whose realization right-thinking people would deem it appropriate to strive.

An idealization, on the other hand, is something quite different. It involves the projection of a hypothesis that removes some limit or limitation of the real (a perfectly elastic body, for example, or a utopia comprised only of sensible and honest people). An idealization is accordingly a thought-instrument—a hypothetical state of things that it may be profitable to think about, but towards whose actual realization in practice it may be altogether senseless to work for. And so, while idealization can prove helpful in theoretical matters, in practical matters it can often do damage.

Ideals, in sum, are constructively action-guiding, while idealizations need by no means be so. A world of eternal springtime might be nice to have if we could get it. But it makes no sense to expend effort and energy in this direction. A positively evaluated idealization does not necessarily constitute a valid ideal.

This distinction between ideals and idealizations bears directly and informatively on the status and standing of consensus. For there is no doubt that consensus is merely an idealization—and neither a sensible goal nor a plausible guide for action, seeing that it prescinds from the variety, diversity, and dissonance that inevitably characterizes the beliefs, opinions, goals, and values of any sizable human community. And so, the fact that consensus represents an idealization does not in and of itself mean that consensus is a valid ideal even when seen in its most positive aspect—that it is something whose pursuit in practice is reasonable and appropriate.

The notion that consensus is a valid ideal—that the endeavour to bring about a uniformity of thought and opinion is an unqualifiedly good thing—is deeply problematic. Consensus is not in general a goal whose pursuit should regulate the way in which we actually proceed in the conduct of our cognitive and practical affairs. In many contexts the interests of the entire community are best served by a fragmentation of beliefs and values within its ranks. For example, the social welfare of a group is usually most effectively catered to when different political sub-units can, though pursuing different policies and adopting different programmes, provide testing grounds for the evaluation of alternatives. And the communal welfare of a group is generally more effectively served when different religious or cultural 'sects' or 'schools of thought' that can provide a congenial home for individuals with different personal needs and inclination. Consensus can be the cause of boredom, inaction, stagnation, and complacency. It can result in a narrowing of horizons and a diminution of options that is destructively stultifying—that substitutes bland uniformity for an envigorating variety.

To be sure, in matters of practical decision at the individual and social level consensus can be a significant desideratum. Our mind is eased if the consulting physicians can agree in a diagnosis and course of treatment, for then we have done all we can to put dissonant possibilities out of range. The climate of public opinion is advantaged when the representatives of different interests and points of view can reach a meeting of minds, for then the likelihood of social conflict is minimized. But of course fate is not generally all that co-operative; agreement in such matters is not so common that we have a right to expect it. A well-designed social order has to be able to make do without consensus.

And this is just as true for matters of value and feeling as it is for matters of belief. Granted, a shared stance on matters of evaluation and sentiment is a desideratum that facilitates social interaction. It fosters social cohesion for people to agree regarding the objects of fear, awe, admiration, etc. No doubt our comfort level is higher among kindred spirits. But the fact remains that a modern society moves beyond all prospects of tribal cohesion in its inevitable complexity. In contemporary conditions a benign social system must make room for diversity and variation—be it social, cultural, political, or religious. Effective social engineering must here foster a good prospect for tolerance, acceptance, and collaboration in the face of diversity. Acquiescence in difference becomes a prime desideratum and peaceful co-existence despite dissensus is desirable to the point of being necessary.

To appreciate the proper place of consensus in the scheme of things, we do well to bear in mind the general difference between a limited-purpose *desideratum* and a general *requirement* (a *sine qua non*) for the achievement of social rationality. Here, as elsewhere, there is a crucial difference between being desirable (having a place on the register of positive factors) and being essential (having so high a place on this register that all or most other considerations should yield way). Even at best, consensus can qualify for no more than the former status.

The situation differs in this regard as between theoretical and practical philosophy. A resort to idealization in theoretical philosophy—in matters of inquiry, truth, and rationality—is something of a harmless bit of theoretical ornamentation. But in matters of practical philosophy idealization can do actual harm. No doubt, ideals can be a useful motive in the direction of positive action. But generally only as a *primum mobile*—an initiator. To hold to the hard and fast, in season and out—not just at the start of the process of decision and action but all along the line—can be dangerous and self-defeating. By diverting our attention away from the attainable realities, a preoccupation with the unrealizable ideal can do real damage in this domain where a pursuit of the unrealizable best can all too easily get in the way of the realization of attainable betterments and impede the achievement of realizable positive objectives. It might be nice for me to be a good polo player but if this lies beyond my means and talents, it would be foolish to let this desideratum get in the way of my perfectly feasible and attainable goal of being a good tennis player. It would be a splendid thing to be a great artist, but for many individuals it would be counter-productive to let this aspiration get in the way of being a good craftsman. Similarly it might be nice to have social consensus, but it would be counter-productive to let this get in the way of social amelioration—of effecting various smaller, but perfectly feasible improvements in the arrangements of a pluralistically diversified society. In so far as consensus is something positive, it has to be seen in the light of a desideratum rather than a valid aspiration of the sort at issue with an ideal.

What then, is the overall assessment of consensus in the light of the present deliberations? The response has to be one that is highly qualified and nuanced. For our considerations combine to indicate that

consensus is not a criterion of truth
   is not a standard of value
   is not an index of moral or ethical appropriateness
   is not a requisite for co-operation
   is not a communal imperative for a just social
   order
   is not, in and of itself, an appropriate ideal

All in all, our position is a markedly guarded one that downgrades consensus both as a theoretical standard and as a practical requisite. Consensus—so we have seen—is no more than one positive factor that has to be weighed on the scale along with many others.

Seen in this light, consensus can be viewed as an inherently limited good much like money. It has the character of being something one would welcome having if it can be secured—in the right way—by fair means and 'at the right price'. Yet unlike honesty, say, or social justice, it does not merit unqualified approbation and is no proper object of a generalized imperative for its promotion at any and every opportunity.

Bibliography

ALBERT, HANS, *Traktat über kritische Vernunft*, 4th rev. edn., (Mohr: Einheit der Gessellschafts-Wissenschaft, 1980).

APEL, KARL-OTTO, *Transzendentale Traümerei* (Göttingen: Hoffman & Campi, 1975).

—— 'Fallibilismus, Konsenztheorie der Wahrheit und Letztbegründung', in W. R. Köhler, *et al.* (eds.), *Philosophie und Begründung* (Frankfurt am Main: Forum für Philosophie, Bad Homburg; 1987).

—— *Diskurs und Verantwortung* (Frankfurt am Main: Suhrkamp, 1988).

ASCH, SOLOMON, 'Studies of Independence and Conformity; i. A Minority of One Against a Unanimous Majority', *Psychological Monographs: General and Applied*, 70 (1956).

BENHABIB, S., and DALLMAYER, F. (eds.), *The Communicative Ethic Controversy* (Cambridge, Mass.: MIT Press, 1990).

BERLIN, ISAIAH, *Four Essays on Liberty* (Oxford: Oxford University Press, 1969).

—— 'The Apotheosis of the Romantic Will', in *The Crooked Timber of Humanity: Studies in the History of Ideas* (London: John Murray, 1990).

BLACK, DUNCAN, *The Theory of Committees and Elections* (Cambridge: Cambridge University Press, 1958).

BRAND, ARIE, *The Force of Reason: An Introduction to Habermas' Theory of Communicative Action* (London: Allen & Unwin, 1990).

BRENTANO, MARGHERITA VON, 'Wissenschaftspluralismus', *Das Argument*, 13 (1971), 476–93.

CAMPBELL, RICHMOND, and SNOWDEN, LANNING, *Paradoxes of Rationality and Co-operation: Prisoner's Dilemma and Newcomb's Problem* (Vancouver: University of British Columbia Press, 1985), [7–30].

DAVIDSON, DONALD, 'On the Very Idea of a Conceptual Scheme', *Proceedings and Addresses of the American Philosophical Association*, 47 (1973–4), 5–20.

DETTLING, WARNFRIED, 'Grenzen des Pluralismus' in Gerd Langguth (ed.), *Aspekte der Reformpolitik* (Mainz: Hase u. Koehler, 1971), 49–65.

DIEMER, ALOYS (ed.), *Der Methoden- und Theorienpluralismus in den Wissenschaften* (Düsseldorf: Philosophisches Institut der Universität Düsseldorff, 1971).

FEYERABEND, P. K., *Against Method: Outline of an Anarchistic Theory of Knowledge* (London: New Left Books, 1975; 2nd rev. edn., London: Verso, 1978).

FISHWICK, MARSHALL W., *Lee After the War* (Westport, Conn.: Greenwich Press, 1963).

FLOWER, ELIZABETH, and MURPHEY, MURRAY G., *A History of Philosophy in America* (New York: Putnam, 1977).

GALTUNG, JOHANN, 'Pluralismus und die Zukunft der menschlichen Gesellschaft', in Dieter Senghaas (ed.), *Kritische Friedensforschung* (Frankfurt am Main: Suhrkamp Verlag, 1971), 164–231.

GAUTHIER, DAVID, *The Logic of Leviathan* (Oxford: Clarendon Press, 1969).
—— 'Constituting Democracy', in *Lindley Lecture Series* (Kansas City: University of Kansas, 1989).

HABERMAS, JÜRGEN, *Zur Logik der Sozialwissenschaften* (Frankfurt am Main: Surkamp Verlag, 1970).
—— 'Vorbereitende Bemerkungen zu einer Theorie der Kommunikativen Kompetenz', in J. Habermas and T. Luhmann (eds.), *Theorie der Gesellschaft oder Sozialtechnologie* (Frankfurt am Main: Suhrkamp Verlag, 1971), 101–41.
—— *Legitimationsprobleme in Spätkapitalismus* (Frankfurt am Main: Suhrkamp Verlag, 1973). Eng. tr. by Thomas McCarthey, *Legitimation Crisis* (Boston: Beacon Press, 1975).
—— 'Was heisst Universalpragmatik?', in K. O. Apel (ed.), *Sprachpragmatik und Philosophie* (Frankfurt am Main: Suhrkamp Verlag, 1976), 174–272.
—— *Zur Rekonstruktion des Historischen Materialismus* (Frankfurt am Main: Suhrkamp Verlag, 1976).
—— 'Wahrheitstheorien', in H. Fahrenbach (ed.), *Wirklichkeit und Reflexion: Festschrift für Walter Schulz* (Pfüllingen: Nerhe Verlag, 1973), 211–65, repr. in G. Skirbekk, *Wahrheitstheorien* (Frankfurt am Main: Suhrkamp Verlag, 1977).
—— *Theorie des kommunikativen Handelns*, 2 vols. (Frankfurt am Main: Suhrkamp Verlag, 1981). i. *Reason and the Rationalization of Society*, tr. Thomas McCarthy (Boston: Beacon Press, 1984); ii. *Lifeworld and System* (Boston: Beacon Press, 1987).
—— *Moralbewusstsein und kommunikatives Handeln* (Frankfurt am Main: Suhrkamp Verlag, 1983). *Moral Consciousness and Communicative Action*, tr. C. Lenhardt and S. W. Nicholsen (Cambridge, Mass.: MIT Press, 1990).
—— *Vorstudien und Ergänzungen zur Theorie des kommunikativen Handelns* (Frankfurt am Main: Suhrkamp Verlag, 1984).
—— *Die neue Unübersichtlichkeit* (Frankfurt am Main: Suhrkamp Verlag, 1985).
—— *Nachmetaphysisches Denken* (Frankfurt am Main: Suhrkamp Verlag, 1988).
—— *Jürgen Habermas on Society and Politics: A Reader*, ed. S. Seidman (Boston: Beacon Press, 1989).

HAMPTON, JEAN, *Hobbes and the Social Contract Tradition* (Cambridge: Cambridge University Press, 1986).

HARRIS, A. R., *Rationality and Collective Belief* (Norwood, NJ: Ellwood, 1986).

HELMER, OLAF, *Looking Forward* (Beverly Hills, Calif.: Sage Publications, 1983).

HONNETH, AXEL, and JOAN, HANS (eds.), *Communicative Action* (Cambridge, Mass.: MIT Press, 1990).

HOPE, V. M., *Virtue by Consensus* (Oxford: Clarendon Press, 1989).

JAMES, WILLIAM, *Pragmatism* (New York: Longmans, Green & Co., 1907).

JANIS, IRVIN LESTER, *Victims of Groupthink* (Boston: Houghton Mifflin, 1972).

KALVEN, HARRY, Jr. and ZEISEL, HANZ, *The American Jury* (Chicago: University of Chicago Press, 1966).

KAVKA, G. *Hobbesian Moral and Political Theory* (Princeton, NJ: Princeton University Press, 1986).

KEKES, JOHN, *A Justification of Rationality* (Albany, NY: SUNY Press, 1976).

—— *The Morality of Pluralism* (Princeton, NJ: Princeton University Press, 1993).

KERFERD, G. B., *The Sophists* (Cambridge: Cambridge University Press, 1981).

KIRK, G. S., RAVEN, J. F., and SCHOFIELD, M., *The Presocratic Philosophers*, 2nd edn. (Cambridge: Cambridge University Press, 1983).

KRÖNER, FRANZ, *Die Anarchie der philosophischen Systeme* (Leipzig: F. Meiner, 1929); repr. (Graz: Akademische Verlagsanstalt, 1972).

KUHLMANN, WOLFGANG, *Reflexive Letztbegründung* (Freiburg: K. Alber, 1985).

KUHN, THOMAS, *The Structure of Scientific Revolutions* (Chicago: University of Chicago Press, 1962; 2nd edn., 1970).

KUKLIK, BRUCE, *The Rise of American Philosophy* (New Haven, Conn., and London: Yale University Press, 1977).

LEHRER, KEITH, and WAGNER, CARL, *Rational Consensus in Science and Society* (Dordrecht: Reidel, 1990).

LENK, HANS, *Philosophie in Technologischen Zeitalter* (Stuttgart: Kohlhammer Verlag, 1971).

LEVY, ISAAC, 'Consensus as Shared Agreement and Outcome of Inquiry', *Synthese*, 62 (1985), 3–11.

MACKAY, ALFRED F., *Arrow's Theorem: The Paradox of Social Choice* (New Haven, Conn., and London: Yale University Press, 1980).

MCCARTHY, THOMAS, *The Critical Theory of Jürgen Habermas* (Cambridge, Mass.: MIT Press, 1978).

—— *Ideals and Illusions: On Reconstruction and Deconstruction in Contemporary Critical Theory* (Cambridge, Mass.: MIT Press, 1991).

MILL, J. S., *Utilitarianism* (London: Longmans Green & Co., 1859).

MOSER, P. K., 'On Scientific Justification by Consensus', *Zeitschrift für allgemeine Philosophie*, 17 (1986).

NAESS, ARNE, 'Pluralistic Theorizing in Physics and Philosophy', *Danish Yearbook of Philosophy*, 1 (1964), 101–11.

—— *The Pluralist and Possibilist Aspect of the Scientific Enterprise* (Oslo: Universitetsverlaget, 1972).

ORTEGA Y GASSET, JOSÉ, *El Espectador* (Madrid: Revista de Occidente, 1916).

—— *Obras* (Madrid: Alianza, 1932).

PARFIT, DEREK, 'Prudence, Morality, and Prisoner's Dilemma', *Proceedings of the British Academy*, 65 (1979), 539–64.

PEIRCE, C. S., *Collected Papers*, 8 vols. (Cambridge, Mass.: Harvard University Press, 1931–58).

PEPPER, STEPHEN C., *World Hypotheses* (Berkeley and Los Angeles: University of California Press, 1942).

POLANYI, MICHAEL, *Personal Knowledge* (Chicago: University of Chicago Press, 1974).

PREUSS, ULRICH, K., *Legalität und Pluralismus* (Frankfurt am Main: Suhrkamp Verlag, 1973).

PRICE, H. H., *Belief* (London: Macmillan, 1969).

PUNTEL, LORENZ, *Grundlagen einer Theorie der Wahrheit* (Berlin: de Gruyter, 1990).

Rawls, John, *A Theory of Justice* (Cambridge, Mass.: Harvard University Press, 1971).

—— 'The Idea of an Overlapping Consensus', *Oxford Journal of Legal Studies*, 7 (1987), 1–25.

RESCHER, NICHOLAS, *Many Valued Logic* (New York: McGraw Hill, 1969).

—— *Induction* (Oxford: Basil Blackwell, 1980).

—— *Scepticism* (Oxford: Basil Blackwell, 1980).

—— *Empirical Inquiry* (Totowa, NJ: Rowman & Littlefield, 1982).

—— *Risk* (Lanham, Md.: University Press of America, 1983).

—— *The Limits of Science* (Berkeley and Los Angeles: University of California Press, 1984).

—— *The Strife of Systems* (Pittsburgh: University of Pittsburgh Press, 1985).

—— *Forbidden Knowledge* (Dordrecht, Boston, London: D. Reidel, 1987).

—— *Rationality* (Oxford: Clarendon Press, 1988).

—— *Baffling Phenomena* (Totowa, NJ: Rowman & Littlefield, 1991).

—— and BRANDOM, ROBERT, *The Logic of Inconsistency* (Oxford: Basil Blackwell, 1980).

RORTY, RICHARD, *Consequences of Pragmatism* (Minneapolis: University of Minnesota Press, 1982).

SABINI, JOHN, and SILVER, MAURY, *Moralities of Everyday Life* (Oxford: Oxford University Press, 1982).

SARKAR, HUSAIN, 'A Theory of Group Rationality', *Studies in History and Philosophy of Science*, 13 (1982), 55–72.

—— *A Theory of Method* (Berkeley and Los Angeles: University of California Press, 1983).

SCHNÄDELBACH, HERBERT (ed.), *Rationalität: Philosophische Beiträge* (Frankfurt am Main: Suhrkamp, 1984).

—— *Vernunft und Geschichte* (Frankfurt am Main; Suhrkamp, 1987).

SCHUMPETER, JOSEF, *Capitalism, Socialism, and Democracy*, 3rd edn. (New York: Houghton Mifflin, 1950).

SIEGEL, HARVEY, *Relativism Refuted* (Dordrecht: Reidel, 1987).

SIMMEL, GEORG, 'Über eine Beziehung der Selektionslehre zur Erkenntnistheorie', in *Archiv für systematische Philosophie und Soziologie*, 1 (1895), 34–45.

SPINNER, HELMUT F., 'Theoretical Pluralism', *Kommunitation*, 4 (1968), 181–201.

—— *Pluralismus als Erkenntnismodell* (Frankfurt am Main: Suhrkamp Verlag, 1974).

STICH, STEPHEN, P., *The Fragmentation of Reason* (Cambridge, Mass.: MIT Press, 1991).

STOCKER, MICHAEL, *Plural and Conflicting Values* (Oxford: Clarendon Press, 1990).

WHITE, STEPHEN, *The Recent Work of Jürgen Habermas* (Cambridge: Cambridge University Press, 1988).

WHORF, BENJAMIN LEE, 'Language and Logic', in *Language, Thought, and*

Reality, ed. J. B. Carroll (Cambridge, Mass.: Harvard University Press, 1956).

WÜSTEHUBE, AXEL, 'Vollständige oder unvollständige Rationalität', *Philosophische Rundschau*, 24 (1991), 257–74.

ZIMMERMAN, RITA, *Die Relevanz einer herrschenden Meinung für Anwendung, Fortbildung und wissenschaftliche Erforschung des Rechts* (Berlin: Dunker & Humblot, 1983).

Index of Names